D1155170

Big Hollow

A Mountaintop History
Maplecrest, Windham, NY

Elwood Hitchcock

BLACK · DOME

Black Dome Press Corp.
RR1, Box 422
Hensonville, NY 12439
Tel: (518) 734-6357
Fax: (518) 734-5802

First Edition, 1993
Published by Black Dome Press Corp.
RR1, Box 422
Hensonville, NY 12439
Tel: (518) 734-6357
Fax: (518) 734-5802

Library of Congress Catalog Card Number: 93-071440

ISBN 0-9628523-7-6

Printed in the USA

Vacationland of Scenic Splendor the Catskill Mts

William Phelp's place (later Dr. Alfred Gundersen's summer home), near today's forest preserve and the source of the Batavia Kill creek, Route 56.

Acknowledgements

Big Hollow would not have been possible without the help of many people who willingly shared information, personal recollections and family pictures with me.

Those to whom I am especially indebted for their generous assistance are Alice Hitchcock Smith, Walter Baker, Ellen Gundersen Wolfe, Marguerite Vining, Leon and Lillian MacGlashan, Winfred and Irene Rickard, Doris Irish Garvey, Larry Tompkins, Patricia H. Davis, Matina Billias, and Carolyn Bennett.

I also offer a note of gratitude to those long dead whose conversations provided much information and inspiration for this book.

To my wife, secretary and helpmate of 54 years, Alvena DeLong Hitchcock, I am overwhelmingly grateful for her inspiration, encouragement and the countless hours she has patiently given to research, picture taking, typing and editing.

Special thanks to the Maplecrest Free Methodist Church for their generous contribution towards this publication. This publication is made possible, in part, with public funds from the Decentralization Program of the NYS Council on the Arts administered in Greene County by the Greene County Council on the Arts with the support of the Town of Windham.

Elwood Hitchcock

East Jewett, New York

INTRODUCTION

IN the remote northeastern corner of the Catskill Mountains is a basin surrounded by high mountains, known as Big Hollow. The basin's only outlet is at the western end of the valley. The Batavia Kill creek flowing through the basin has its source in a little mountain spring at the valley's eastern end.

It was to this lonely, isolated, uninhabited basin of virgin timberland that Deacon Lemuel Hitchcock, his wife Mamre and their nine children came on an ox-sled in the mid-winter of 1795. A crude cabin had been built by Lemuel and his oldest son, Thomas, the previous autumn. Lemuel, who had been a captain in the Revolutionary War, was a religious man, and desired to bring up his children in a spiritual atmosphere.

The pioneer settlers of Big Hollow were families whose parents and children worked together in a spirit of unity for their collective survival. They grew in love for and loyalty to the family, and learned how to live cooperatively with other people. As they worked together under crude conditions, they developed creative thinking and initiative for doing work more easily and better. Also, caring for domestic animals and working outdoors, they developed health and spiritual qualities.

God must have looked down upon his children in the isolated mountain valley and blessed them. It wasn't long before three flourishing churches were established to serve the population of around 200. It appears, too, that God's spirit has hovered over the basin since those years to bless the descendants of the pious pioneers with peace and prosperity.

I, the author of this book, consider myself most fortunate to have lived in Big Hollow, now Maplecrest, the first 30 years of my life. It was a neighborhood of good homes and good people. I write to tell my thoughts and remembrances of my childhood home and of the people I knew.

Contents

THE BEGINNING

THE man and boy were tired even though it was still light. Early that morning they had left their home in the Hudson Valley near Durham and walked south to the foothills of the Northern Catskill Mountains. Then, they climbed the escarpment to the low pass between Windham High Peak and the Ridge Plateau.

As they looked down into the big hollow with the mountains to the south, they were amazed at the primeval forest of tall evergreens and hardwoods. Here they could see that the big basin was enclosed by a high mountain to the north, a plateau to the east and three tall mountain peaks to the south. It was a scene the eyes of no white man had ever before looked upon—a big hollow in the mountains, nearly completely enclosed.

Quickly, father and son descended to the valley floor where they found a little stream of cold mountain water flowing gently toward the west. It seemed like a sacred moment as the man and boy stood entranced by the stream in the silence and grandeur of the mountains. It was early autumn, 1794. The earth was carpeted with brightly covered leaves. The sun threw warm shimmering rays through the forest trees. The air was fragrant and cool. Like Moses of old at the burning bush, this spot seemed like hallowed ground.

The man, his wife, and eight small children had left Cheshire, Connecticut in 1792, looking for a place where he might bring up his children to worship God according to the dictates of his conscience. The father had been born in Cheshire on December 20, 1749, one of six sons. He was the fifth-generation descendant of Matthias Hitchcock, who had come to Boston from London, England in 1635. He had served in the Revolutionary War as a captain and had been paid for his service with Continental currency, which left him a poor man. Later, when given a pension, he signed off his rights to it, as he believed his country needed the money more than he did.

The years between the end of the Revolutionary War and the adoption of the Constitution were difficult for the new nation. They were known as ''the critical period.'' The Articles of Confederation were weak. Nation and colonists were heavily in debt. Homes and property were being lost. The west beckoned to the unhappy, discouraged people. In the Massachusetts Colonies, there was dissension over the strict religious discipline of the Pilgrims and Puritans.

Thomas Hooker, a Puritan minister, led a group of followers to build a settlement near what is now Hartford, Connecticut. It marked the beginning of migration to the west. Later, Roger Williams, another Puritan clergyman, led a group that founded a settlement in Providence, Rhode Island. The Rev. Williams believed there should be no union between the church and state; that people should worship as they choose; and that no one should be punished for not attending religious services or for not contributing to the support of the church.

It was during these critical, unsettled times that Deacon Lemuel Hitchcock migrated with his wife and children westward, across the Hudson River, to the little Durham settlement in the Hudson Valley. But the settlement in 1792 was a disappointment to him. The inhabitants were not of a religious nature. They were Sabbath-breakers with loose moral habits and principles. It was no place to bring up children.

In Durham, Lemuel lifted up his eyes as the Psalmist of old and looked to the south. There he beheld the northern range of the beautiful Catskill Mountains. Somewhere in those mountains he would find a home for his family where they might worship God. So it was, on that autumn day in 1794, that Lemuel and his son Thomas, a lad of 12 years, found themselves downstream about two miles from the source of the Batavia Kill creek in a big mountain hollow.

Standing at the edge of the stream and taking in as much of the grandeur of the countryside as possible, Lemuel exclaimed, ''Here will I stop. Here will I live. And here will I be buried.'' Raising his ax and striking it into a strong tree, he prayed.

The land to the south of the creek was fertile and flat. It would be tillable when free from its dense forest of pines and other timber. The stream abounded with trout. Wild animals prowled through the forest and would provide food and garments. There was a good location for a sawmill.

Father and son went to work with diligence. A crude cabin without floor or doors was soon erected. A square mile of land was marked off extending on both sides of the Batavia Kill and reaching from what is now the Leon MacGlashan property on the east to Lane's Lake on the west.

Very early in the spring of 1795, Lemuel brought his family, including his wife, a feeble woman, children and all their possessions, on an ox-drawn sled to their new mountain home. Only a son, Lemuel II, a puny boy, was left behind, adopted by a family in the Durham settlement.

So it was, the first settler and his family to the Big Hollow in the mountains arrived at the eastern end of the Windham Valley in the early spring of 1795. Six miles down the valley on the Batavia Kill, George Stimson of

Farmingham, Massachusetts had already built a shanty by a big rock in 1785. And about half-way between George Stimson's home in Windham and Deacon Lemuel's in Big Hollow, George Henson, another pioneer, would later establish the Hensonville settlement. Thus, the Town of Windham was settled, and Deacon Lemuel and his family began clearing the forest, putting up buildings and starting life in their new cabin in Big Hollow.

RELIGION IN BIG HOLLOW

DEACON Lemuel was a man of deep spiritual character. He believed that his main purpose in life was to worship God and to bring up his children to be followers of Christ, so he began each day in his home with his family coming together for daily devotions, which included Bible reading, prayer and the singing of a hymn. Throughout the day, Lemuel and his wife Mamre were mindful of their responsibility to instruct their children in godly living by example and precept. The day ended with the family coming together again for prayer before going to bed. On Sundays, Deacon Lemuel would conduct a religious service in his home by reading the sermon of a prominent clergyman, leading in prayer and the singing of hymns. He also would teach his children Sunday school lessons on particular topics and Bible characters.

As the westward movement continued, more pioneers, especially those of a religious nature, heard that Big Hollow in the Catskill Mountains was a desirable place to settle. Deacon Lemuel and his family were honest, upright people. The encircling mountains afforded protection from the forces of nature. Indians didn't inhabit the area. The isolation and remoteness of the place provided safety and serenity. The rich, virgin soil, great forests, wild animals and fish made making a home and living there appealing.

As more immigrants moved into the settlement, some would worship with the Hitchcock family in their cabin on Sunday mornings. As time went on, an itinerant minister occasionally would visit the settlement and conduct Sunday services. An evangelist, now and then, would hold revival meetings in one of the larger cabins for a week or longer.

It soon became obvious that a public place of worship was needed. Deacon Lemuel, being of Scottish descent and a Presbyterian by faith, recommended building a Presbyterian church. There were already Presbyterian churches at Catskill, Ashland, Windham and Jewett.

THE PRESBYTERIAN CHURCH

On December 10, 1822, a meeting of 21 settlers formed the Presbyterian Church Society. The following day, officers were elected and the minutes of a December 15, 1826, meeting lists the membership of the newly-formed church as being 27 adults and 22 children belonging to the Church by baptism.

A meeting house was built for church services and served the settlement for several years before being burned on February 3, 1833. Work was immediately started on a new and larger meeting house, which was completed and dedicated on September 10, 1833, only seven months and seven days later.

Sometime around 1850, a large church was built down in the village below the cemetery to accommodate the growing congregation. This was a large edifice with a sanctuary to seat nearly 200 people. A large platform at the front extended the entire width of the building. The sanctuary was heated by two small wood stoves at the rear of the church and on either side. Their smoke pipes went up nearly to the ceiling and then extended all the way to the front of the church and into the two outside chimneys. At the rear of the sanctuary there was also a small room on each side of the entrance hallway for Sunday school classes and for storage. A stairway led from these rooms to a balcony where another 50 people could be seated. At the rear of the balcony was a doorway leading to the belfry. The bell was large and weighed nearly half a ton. It took a large gang of men with ropes, tackles and poles to raise it to its position in the steeple.

At the rear of the building there was a large horse shed divided into many sections for the horses and wagons of the parishioners on Sundays. This church was to serve the people of Big Hollow for many years. Some of the people and children who came to Sunday school during later years were Bertha, Fredonia and Vernette Moseman, Alda Bray, Claude Van, Walter Baker and Leonard Vining.

As the years went by, the membership and attendance of the old church declined. The older members died; the young went away to school or married and moved to other communities. Then, too, the Methodist Church and Free Methodist Church were becoming well-established with a newer and larger membership.

The old church had never had a resident pastor, but shared one with the Ashland and Windham Presbyterian Churches. As attendance dropped off, it was decided to terminate the worship service and attend one of the other churches for this service. The Sunday school continued for a short time longer, then that, too, was closed. Then in 1948, the officers deeded the church over to the Free Methodist Society. This was a fitting and gracious gesture as the Free Methodist parsonage was next to the church building and many of that membership were close neighbors, friends and descendants of Deacon Lemuel. The building now stands tall and beautiful with additional classrooms, a well-equipped sanctuary, and a large, active membership.

Beers, in his *History of Greene County*, refers to the Big Hollow Presbyterian Church, the second Presbyterian Church of Windham, as having been active in benevolent and Christian work, a church that had been a constant and liberal contributor to foreign missions and charitable causes, and a church that had perpetuated and reflected the spirit of Deacon Lemuel Hitchcock, a pioneer of Big Hollow.

THE METHODIST CHURCH

Little is known of Bethuel Barnum (1820-1893), his ancestry or where he came from. He was a farmer and a dedicated Methodist with a large family. He had moved to an old farm on the north side of the mountain near the upper end of the valley. Bethuel and his first wife, Phoebe Shoemaker, had nine children. Sometime after her death in 1864, at the age of 49, he married his second wife, Mary Bunt, and they became the parents of eight children. Of Bethuel's 17 children, seven grew up and settled in Big Hollow and four others in the neighboring community of East Jewett.

Bethuel Barnum was the founder of Methodism in Big Hollow and he, his children and their families were the core of the church from the time it was organized and built in 1857 and '58 until the 1920's, a period of over 60 years. In 1878, the Maplecrest Church united with the Methodist Churches of Hensonville and East Jewett and became known as the Hensonville Charge. This Hensonville Charge of the three churches still exists today.

Bethuel's children who remained in Big Hollow and had families were Stewart, Jabez, Emma Crandell, Sarah Brainard, Julia Rickard, Levi and Martin Barnum. The East Jewett residents were David, George, John and Clara Beach.

Jabez (1862-1923), the youngest son of Bethuel and Phoebe, was a natural leader, gifted, industrious and versatile. He and his wife, Elizabeth Bray, became the parents of six children: Olin, Walter, William, Ralph, Frances and Julia.

Among Jabez's many activities were those of stone mason, building chimneys, erecting stone smokehouses and doing concrete work. He was a good farmer and enlarged his house to become a summer resort hotel for city guests. He was one of the first in Big Hollow to own a gasoline engine for sawing wood and threshing oats and buckwheat. A musician, he could sing and play nearly any musical instrument. He taught his sons to play, purchased instruments for them and formed a Barnum Band with Sam West playing the fife.

Being a dedicated and faithful Christian, he was a strong leader and diligent worker in his Methodist Church, serving over the years as a trustee, Sunday school superintendent and teacher.

Among other faithful and loyal members of the church were Emma Crandell, Jabez's sister and a long-remembered Sunday school teacher; Romaine Law, organist and teacher; Jacob and Ella Planck; Sidney and Kate Van; John and

Alice Haynes; Amy and Julia Rickard; Claudia Bray and daughter Alda; Mrs. William Henry Moseman, son Sherwood, and his three daughters Fredonia, Bertha and Vernette; George MacGlashan and family; George's son Leon MacGlashan and Lillian and family; Martin Barnum and family and others. In the early 1920's, Val and Irene Morrow moved into the community and became leaders and dedicated workers in the church.

Between 1940 and 1970, the church made great progress. In 1946, a total of 18 members were taken in. Also during this period, an addition of 15 feet by 50 feet was added to the rear of the church. Eight beautiful stained glass windows were installed. In 1959, Edward MacGlashan built 18 oak pews for the sanctuary and in 1967, Sterling Planck presented the church with a new Hammond organ in memory of his grandfather, Jabez Barnum.

On Sunday, June 14, 1981, there was a Methodist Homecoming Reunion at the church with more than 100 members and friends of the church present to enjoy the service, luncheon and to renew friendships.

Pleasant memories were recalled of Christmas programs with children and young people singing and of the tall brightly lit Christmas tree; of mid-week prayer meetings in the homes of the Vans, Crandells, Plancks and Rickards; of Sunday evening services in the summer with young people attending from the Thompson House and other resorts; of Church suppers in various homes during the winter months; and of church lawn sales and rummage sales. Although the reminiscences were pleasant, there was also a rather sad and nostalgic feeling at the homecoming.

As the years of the present century sped by, economic and social changes came about. People moved away and church attendance declined. Finally, the Maplecrest Methodist and Hensonville Methodist churches merged into a union church known as the Hensonville-Maplecrest Church at Hensonville. The one big stone (17 3/4 feet long and 4 1/2 feet wide) in front of the church and reaching from the church steps to the street sidewalk remains intact and unused as the doors of the empty church are now closed.

THE FREE METHODIST CHURCH

The Big Hollow Free Methodist Society was an outgrowth of a Free Methodist Class in North Settlement, which held meetings under the leadership of the Rev. George Edwards as early as 1869. Rev. Edwards was filled with a divine fire to proclaim the gospel of holiness anytime and anywhere. He held meetings in Eastkill, Tannersville, Windham and Big Hollow.

Later, services were held in Windham and continued there for about 25 years as it was a central location with members attending from both North Settlement and Big Hollow. Familiar names which appeared at this early date are those of John Howard, Harrison Coons and Wilbur M. Finch.

The Big Hollow Society was organized on June 24, 1871 by the Rev. George Edwards with 24 members. Among them were Mr. and Mrs. John MacGlashan, Mr. and Mrs. Stephen Pierce, Mr. and Mrs. Nelson Hitchcock, Monroe Mallory, Holmes Barker and Sylvester Winchell.

For a time, services were held in schoolhouses, private homes, groves, and barns. It was said that services were occasionally held in a building of Nelson Hitchcock's west of the village, which at one time had been a blacksmith shop.

During the pastorate of Rev. George Eakins, a small church was built at the eastern end of the village in 1875. Land for the building was donated by charter member John MacGlashan, who lived near the end of the village. Mr. MacGlashan also served as boss carpenter. With the assistance of Frank and Norris Cook of Jewett, both of whom donated their labor, he constructed the church. The building was simple and crude, of rough lumber. The seats had no backs. There was no musical instrument. Some 25 years were to pass before a parsonage was erected (around 1900) during the pastorate of the Rev. J.E. Payne.

The early Free Methodists adhered strictly to the doctrines of John Wesley and the first Methodists. They dressed simply and plainly. The women wore long dresses with no adornments, such as rings, jewelry or necklaces—not even a wedding ring. The ministers dressed in dark clerical garb. It was once reported that an elder visiting the church was denied admission because he was wearing a necktie.

The Sabbath was strictly observed. Members were expected to attend all church services and special meetings. Generous giving was required to pay the minister's salary, church expenses and the missionary program.

Free Methodist ministers were humble, dedicated, hardworking people. They preached and taught the Bible by word and example: "Precept upon precept; line upon line; here a little; and there a little," Isaiah 28:10. They preached twice on Sunday and possibly taught a Sunday school class; held weekly prayer meetings; arranged special week-day services and revivals; visited their parishioners and the sick; performed marriage ceremonies and conducted funerals; attended conferences; kept records and spent much time in their office in prayer and study. They were busy, serious men of the cloth with an important mission to perform in saving souls.

There were years in the early church when it was a struggle to keep the church going. At one time, three faithful women—Mary Moseman, Emma Phelps and Frankie Osborn—kept the doors open and the altar warmed with their prayers, work and sacrificial giving.

Over the years, great men of God served the church as its pastors. Evangelists conducted great revival meetings, which kept the spiritual life of the church strong.

As the family of Deacon Lemuel became leaders in the Presbyterian Church, and those of Bethuel Barnum in the Methodist Church, it came about that the family of Lemuel Hitchcock, grandson of Deacon Lemuel, became leaders and workers in the Free Methodist Church. Lemuel and his wife Sarah had four sons—John, George, Charles and Anson; also four daughters—Frankie Osborn, Dell Lewis, Jessie Vining and Minnie Baker Palmer. John died at an early age, but the other seven children grew up in Big Hollow, married and, with the exception of Charlie, established homes and remained there as long as they lived. Their children and grandchildren also became faithful and dedicated members of the church over the years and remained in the locality.

At present, the Rev. Donald Baker, who is pastor of the church, is the sixth generation descendant of Deacon Lemuel as is his cousin Gilbert Vining, who is treasurer and a leader in the church. A great many of the present parishioners can trace back their ancestry to the founder of Big Hollow.

In recent years, great improvements and expansion projects have enlarged and beautified the building which was the old Presbyterian Church and which was deeded to the Free Methodist Church in 1948. The sanctuary has been refurbished with new pews, windows, carpeting and equipment. During the ministry of Rev. A. Lewis Payne, an addition was built to provide more room for the Sunday school. The Living Faith Fellowship Hall, a large building (100 feet by 80 feet) across the street from the church, was acquired in the late 1970's to provide facilities for a youth center, group gatherings and office facilities.

In addition to great revival meetings and religious services over the years, there also have been other events of significance. The 50th annual conference of the New York Conference was held in Maplecrest on September 19-23, 1923. On April 26-29, 1945, Superintendent Rev. Elmer S. Root held a district conference at the church with nearly 100 in attendance. The Roberts College choir gave a concert at the church in 1946. From time to time, District Youth groups have held weekend rallies at the Maplecrest Church and singers and musicians have given concerts on many occasions.

The church over the years has sent numerous young people out into the world in Christian service. Clyde VanValin, son of Ernest and Josephine VanValin and a grandson of John Howard, is a bishop in the Free Methodist Church; his brother John served as a missionary to the Congo, as a pastor, and at present is a superintendent in the church. Donald Baker has served the church for 38 years as a pastor; Marith Reinertsen Bicksler with her husband William is a missionary to Taiwan; Irving Parsons is a retired Free Methodist pastor; Janet Stewart Snyder is the wife of a Free Methodist district superintendent and Josephine Speenburg Tompkins worked for many years as a missionary among the poor people of Crewe, Virginia. Gilbert Vining Jr. and Ronald Vining, sons of Gilbert and Roberta Vining and seventh-generation descendants of Deacon Lemuel, are both in the Lord's ministry.

The church has grown spiritually and in many other ways since its humble inception in 1871. At present it is one of the largest and strongest

Protestant churches in Greene County, with a membership of 76 and an average Sunday morning attendance of more than 80.

The three small churches of Big Hollow were all active in the little settlement for more than 60 years. On Sundays, families gathered in each church to worship God and to have fellowship with one another. Seldom did a winter blizzard or a summer storm prevent a Sunday service. On special occasions, such as a wedding or the funeral of a neighbor or a child the whole community came together as one big family in one church for the service.

Although there was diversity among the three churches in denominational doctrine, there also was a strong bond of love which in turn developed a spirit of unity. Fortunate, indeed, were those residents who lived in such a Christian atmosphere, in a community where there was no theater, no dance hall, no bar, and with very little crime of any kind. Fortunate, indeed, were those children and young people who grew up in such a spiritual and moral climate.

THE BIG HOLLOW SCHOOLS

CHRISTIANITY has always encouraged education. The Pilgrims and Puritans established schools that their children might learn to read the Bible. The first colleges and universities in the Colonies were founded by religious denominations: Harvard, Princeton and Syracuse by the Methodists; Bucknell, by the Baptists; Hartwick, by the Lutherans; and Roberts, by the Free Methodists. Churches founded colleges to train young people for the ministry, to become missionary workers, and for Christian service.

In Big Hollow, as in other settlements, parents were the first teachers and their cabin the first schoolhouse for their children. Later, as more settlers moved into the valley, a crude schoolhouse was built with a big fireplace at one end. As time went on a more modern building replaced this original one.

Tradition indicates that the first schoolhouse was at the junction of the Ridge Road and the road on the north side of the Batavia Kill creek, opposite what was long known as the Chatfield house. Raymond Moseman, a local teacher, once taught in that school and had as pupils Louise and Willis Chatfield; Louis, David and George Irish; Lucy Crandell; and Robert and Bessie Peck. The three Irish brothers lived about a mile up the Ridge Road.

As more people moved into the eastern end of the basin, a new school was built near the junction of the Ruland road and the main road, a short distance above the Jabez Barnum home. This school was in operation until the 1930's. Ellen MacGlashan, a local resident, and Birdsell Moseman, Raymond Moseman's son, were among the last teachers before the school was closed and became a part of the WAJ Centralized School District. Other teachers in this district during the early 1900's were Walter Pelham, Marguerite Winchell Peck, Norma Winchell Soper, all of Hensonville; also a Rev. Sharpe and Scott Vining. Among the pupils who attended this school were Robert and Beulah Newcomb, Sterling Planck, Doris Irish, Lois Irish, Emma Planck, Lawrence Peck and Evelyn and Lillian Crandell.

Marguerite Peck remembers often walking the four miles from her Hensonville home to and from school. Sometimes she drove a horse or rode a bicycle. In bad weather she would stay over at the Jabez Barnum home. In those days school began at nine o'clock and ended at four.

THE LOWER BIG HOLLOW SCHOOL DISTRICT

A third location became necessary for a school as the population center shifted down the valley to where the village was developing. Here were the store and post office, blacksmith shop, three churches, a shoe repairman (John Irish), private homes and, later, a creamery.

The school was built about a quarter of a mile below the village on the Hensonville Road and near the Batavia Kill creek. Across the road from the school, under the roots of a big hemlock tree, was a spring which flowed into the creek. At the rear of the school there was a large playground area and behind that a rather steep bank with a brook flowing at its base in the springtime. Double outdoor toilets were built just west of the school.

The location was ideal for a school and playground. The field was large enough for baseball and other games. The creek offered good trout fishing, skating in the winter and floating on cakes of ice in the spring. The brook also made a good place to skate and coast in winter and in the spring could be dammed up for a big, deep pond between its banks near the Garvey house on the west. The long high hill behind the school and extending up to the village made riding down hill on a sled a thrilling experience—especially when there was a hard crust and the brook was frozen over. Sometimes, we would take our sleds to school and leave them there over night for a week or longer when the coasting was at its best.

My aunt, Rose Hitchcock, taught school here and my mother Grace Crandell and my wife's father Merritt DeLong were among her pupils. My father and many of his generation went to this school. I was enrolled there in 1915 and continued until 1922 when I entered Windham High School. My brothers Edwin and Wilfred, and our only sister Eva, went to this school.

The school was a one-room building with three windows on each side and one at the rear behind the teacher's desk. There was a row of double seats and desks each side of the room with a bench in front of the teacher's desk for class recitations. Behind the recitation desk in the center of the room stood a large wood stove. Here on cold mornings we would hover around to get warm and to thaw out our ink bottles on top of the stove. Occasionally, a bottle would break or a cork fly high into the air, but this didn't happen often.

School started each morning with a Bible reading, then standing for the Lord's Prayer, Pledge of Allegiance, and the singing of several songs from books all had purchased. Recitations began for the day with the younger children coming up to the teacher's desk, standing beside her one by one as they read orally the assigned lesson for the day. They also learned a few spelling words and some simple basic arithmetic examples.

The one or two children in grades seven and eight would have their lessons just before noon and late in the afternoon. They were usually good pupils who wanted to be well-prepared to take the Regents examinations at Windham and go on to high school there. Eighth-grade Regents examinations were offered in arithmetic, history, geography, English and spelling.

One year, we brought axes, saws, hammers, and nails from home, cut brush between the road and the creek and built a big brush play house. Another time we built a foot bridge over the Batavia Kill creek so we could play baseball on the other side on Uncle Ros Vining's field.

Other popular activities at the school were games such as Keely Over, played by throwing the ball over the schoolhouse; Red Rover; Prisoner's Base; and Fox and Geese in the big field above the school.

Baseball was a game we never tired of playing. We had crude paraphernalia to play with. A boy had made a bat at home from a sapling. A couple of old balls had been made usable with bicycle tape. Several old gloves had been located somewhere. But we chose up teams and played from early spring until the snow came in autumn. One spring, we couldn't wait for the snow to melt on the little diamond, so we brought shovels from home and cleared the field of snow.

We became such good players that a Windham team challenged us to a Saturday afternoon game. Those of us who had bicycles rode them with a player riding on the handlebars or carrier to the neighboring village five miles away . We would have done fairly well and might even have won the game had it not been for one particular Windham player, the pitcher Eddie Stead. He had terrific speed and, unfortunately for us, poor control. We were so scared when we stepped up to the plate, we were unable to concentrate on hitting the ball. We lost the game ingloriously. The game, however, attracted so much attention in the town that the local newspaper wrote an account of it referring to our team as the ''Big Hollow Bat Busters.''

It was during my first year of school in Big Hollow that I experienced for the first time the terrible feeling of not being wanted. It was during the noon hour. We had crossed the creek on our home-made bridge to play ball in Uncle Ros's field. Two of the older boys stood apart to choose sides for the game. The rest of us stood between them waiting to be chosen. Of course, the best players were snapped up first, then the younger, poorer ones were reluctantly taken. Finally, I stood there alone, so terribly alone. The captain whose turn it was to choose said, ''I don't want Elwood.'' The other leader shouted, ''If you don't want him, we don't want him either.'' I was stunned, seemingly paralyzed! Then, the third party who is always present at such times, shouted, ''Come on, let's play ball. We're wasting time.'' Away they went. I stood alone, paralyzed, trying to stifle my sobs.

Slowly, I shuffled off to a little hill and lay down in the warm noon-time sunshine to watch the game. And then I felt someone near me. I opened my tear-filled eyes. It was the teacher. "Elwood," he whispered, "you don't feel well, do you? Wouldn't you like to go home for the afternoon?" "Yes, yes, I would," I cried out. "Get your lunch pail. I know your mother will make you feel better," he said. I went home feeling better. I shall never forget Raymond Moseman. He was a compassionate, understanding teacher. Later, I became an outstanding high-school baseball player, winning the Greene County Championship in 1927 for base running.

The one-room rural school was a great educational institution in the early history of our country. In 1912, there were 11,777 school districts in New York State, most of them, one-room school districts. These early schools were taught by young men and women of character with only a high-school education or less. Sometimes there would be 20 to 30 pupils aged six to 16 in all eight grades in the school. But order was maintained and children learned. Lessons were heard over and over again as a pupil progressed from one grade to another—hearing the children recite in other grades. Two governors, state legislators and bishops began their education in the one-room schools in the town of Windham. I'm glad I had the benefit of attending such a school and later the opportunity to teach in two for six years.

THE EARLY TWENTIETH CENTURY

SINCE Big Hollow was a remote basin with only one outlet, there were few visitors to the wilderness valley. In the Hollow, there was no hotel, restaurant, entertainment hall, bus station or saloon. There were, however, three churches, two one-room schools, a blacksmith shop for shoeing horses and oxen and doing iron work on wagons and sleighs, and a shoemaker who also could mend leather harnesses for horses. You also could find a post office and a general store, which carried a great variety of necessary goods, such as salt; molasses; patent medicines and laxatives; cloth, thread, boots and shoes; kerosene oil, nails, axes and hammers; and some hard candy.

Big Hollow was made up of 26 little village homes and 25 small farm homes with good industrious people. Some people had settled in the Hollow because of its Christian atmosphere. Others came because it was a safe, pleasant place to live. And still others just wanted a more quiet, peaceful setting for their homes.

The Christian homes and the churches with Sunday schools and mid-week prayer meetings exerted a powerful and abiding influence on the population. It was a good place for children. There were few bad people, although there was a report that a counterfeit ring once operated for a short time in a cave on the Ridge Road between East Windham and Big Hollow. Another story that circulated was of an angry farmer who threw his little black slave boy into a quicksand pit when he failed to bring the cows to the barn at night. These fanciful stories, however, were never verified.

It is rather unique and unusual that in nearly two hundred years this little settlement has never had a serious crime such as murder or a natural catastrophe like an earthquake or flood. It has been and still is a quiet, safe and secure place to live.

The economy of the early twentieth century did not require much of an income. Most families were nearly self-sufficient. In the Hollow, there were small farms with from six to thirty dairy cows, a meadow for hay and other crops, a wood lot, summer pasture land and a maple bush. The farmer derived a small income from the sale of milk and perhaps the sale of potatoes in the autumn. He also sold maple syrup and sugar from his maple bush to the village residents in Windham and Hensonville. Sometimes, too, he sold a quarter of beef or half of a dressed pig, but this provided a meager and uncertain income and involved a lot of hard work at extra expense. Often in the autumn, there was an opportunity to work on town roads (and even use one's team of horses for drawing stone).

As for the other families in the Hollow, both in the village and up through the Valley, they, too, lived much as their neighboring farmers, except that they worked during the summer months as carpenters, gardeners and handymen at Onteora Park or the summer resorts in the Hunter-Tannersville Valley.

Sid Van was such a man. He was big, with large hands and a loud voice which indicated confidence and authority. No one knew much about Mr. Van's early life, except that he boasted of coming to the valley from Spruceton, over in the Westkill Valley near Lexington. He delighted in telling about a dog over there that would go alone at night after the cows and bring them to the barn for milking. On one occasion when the cows didn't all come, he returned to the pasture and finally located them several miles away. They had broken down the fence and run away to a neighbor's farm. The dog picked out all of his master's cows from the neighbor's herd and brought them back over the mountain to their own home.

During the summer months, Mr. Van drove his horse and light wagon to Onteora Park or Tannersville, where he had employment as a gardener or repairman. In the winter he would cut wood and draw it with his horse to the woodshed to be piled and stored. Wood was the only fuel used for heating and cooking, except for kerosene oil stoves which were considered dangerous and expensive and used only in the summer for cooking.

The Vans' sons, Danny, Vernon, and Claude, learned well the lesson of diligence from their parents. Vernon, the middle son, worked for us for a number of years. He was an early riser, dependable, and pleasant. For several months we had a milking dairy of 30 cows. Vernon and my father milked these cows twice a day by hand. Sometimes Vernon finished his 15 first. Claude, the youngest son, worked at different jobs for some time. He finally became a truck driver and drove a tractor-trailer for most of his life.

Whenever anyone asked Mr. Van if he could do work such as building a chimney or laying up a wall, whether he had ever done it or not, he always replied, "Yes, sir, and I'll be glad to do the job for you." He knew he could learn to do any kind of work with his hands. Later in life, Mr. Van and Henry Slater went into the construction business together. They had a Steward truck and a concrete mixer, with a small engine to run it , and employed several men. They had work for several years building concrete walks, swimming pools, and cellars for new houses.

There were few people in the community who were more spiritual than Sid and Kate Van. They were dedicated Methodists, faithful at church services and mid-week prayer meetings. Next to their family the church had top priority. Mrs. Van taught Sunday school class, read the Bible to Sid, who came to know it well, and had mid-week prayer meetings in their home as it was centrally located.

At the prayer sessions it was customary to kneel at the chair where one was sitting. Voluntary prayers were made in praise and thanksgiving to God, and petitions were requested for direction and encouragement and for neighborhood needs. Mr. Van prayed with deep feeling and sincerity. He prayed in a loud, senatorial voice and had the habit of adding "uh-uh" to some words to give them emphasis, such as, "Heaven uh-uh, Satan uh-uh, and angels uh-uh." The young people often had difficulty restraining an outburst of laughter while Mr. Van prayed.

Coming home from school one night, I stopped to see Mr. Van who had been sick for some time. It was obvious that he was very ill, but he knew me. I observed that he was picking at the covers over him with his hands. Mrs. Van pulled me to one side and whispered that action was a sure sign the person was dying. A few days later, Mr. Van died. Several years later, Mrs. Van followed him.

Sid and Kate Van I shall never forget. They were simple, uneducated, hardworking people, good friends, good neighbors and righteous in the eyes of all who knew them.

There were other families in the village who lived much like the Vans. These included Henry and Amy Rickard, who lived across from the Sugar Maples office, and George and Julia Rickard, whose home was below the bridge. George grew delicious strawberries and raspberries for which there was great demand. He also owned and operated a cider mill. In the winter months, he overindulged in cold hard cider which brought shame and disgrace to him and Julia, his wife. Fortunately, he gave up hard cider several years before he died.

Henry Osborn and his wife, Frankie, at the upper end of the village also produced much of their own food and fuel, and Henry worked out enough during the summer months to earn money for his taxes and the necessities which he could not produce.

Charlie and Frankie Garvey and two children who lived on the road to East Jewett; Charlie Haddon and his wife; George Ruland and his wife; Ben DeLong and his wife Dessie; Sam West and his wife; and my Grandparents Billy and Emma Crandell, all made a fairly good living without having much of an income. My grandmother, however, did take summer city guests and made butter, which brought in some money for them.

INDUSTRIES OF BIG HOLLOW

WITH all the conveniences and labor-saving devices of the twentieth century, it is difficult to understand the amount of hard work necessary even to exist in early colonial days. Building a crude cabin was a back-breaking, time-consuming job. The settlers had to find the right kind of timber of a uniform size for the sides of the cabin. These logs had to be cut down with an ax, cut to the proper lengths and hauled to the cabin site. Next came the erecting of a frame, stacking the logs one above another, filling in the cracks and making openings for a door and windows. After the roof was on, a fireplace and chimney would be constructed, which would require a great quantity of stone and rock, and hours and days of hard labor.

Other buildings would be required, such as an outdoor toilet, a hen house, pig pen and barn to house a horse, perhaps a couple of cows, some sheep and a loft for hay storage during the winter months. The construction of these buildings with simple, crude tools would take months of hard work, and sometimes years before they were adequately completed.

Meanwhile, the daily work would continue: cutting wood, drawing water, clearing land, planting a garden and other crops, and securing food by hunting, fishing and other means.

The housewife, too, would be overwhelmed with her daily routine—keeping wood on the fire, trying to keep the hard earthen floor clean and warm with skins or blankets, maintaining the family in clothing, doing the mending, and occasionally washing the clothes. Then, too, simple meals had to be prepared in the huge kettle over the fire or on the spit above the open fire. The cabin had to be kept warm night and day in winter. There was little that could be done when illness struck, however. Sickness and death were common and expected, and accepted in early colonial days. They were a part of life.

During the nineteenth century, there was a great development of the natural resources in the Hollow. Giant hemlocks provided bark for tanneries and logs for the sawmills along the Batavia Kill, as did the pine and basswood trees. The maples and beech were ideal for fuel.

In the latter part of the nineteenth century, big lumber wagons with iron-tired wheels were drawing quantities of choice virgin lumber out of the basin to neighboring villages where new homes were being built. Other wagons pulled by horses and oxen were hauling firewood to be sold to public buildings, stores and homes in Hensonville and Windham. The Hollow was beginning to prosper.

As the population increased, the need arose for a blacksmith shop for shoeing horses and oxen, also for shaping iron for wagons and sleighs. There was work for a shoemaker and repairman.

A stone quarry on Elm Ridge opened up to make available stone for sidewalks, curbing, horse blocks and even vaults for cemetery graves.

As the twentieth century began, much of the mountainsides were denuded of the tall, beautiful hemlocks and pines. The choice lumber had mostly disappeared. In its place were acres of cleared land. Here was pasture for cattle and sheep to graze on and meadow for hay and other farm crops. The Hollow was being transformed from a place of tanneries, sawmills and lumbering to an area of small farms, with large hay and dairy barns, hen houses, pig pens and big houses for big families.

The building of the railroads into the mountains and the Otis Elevated Railroad opened up the mountain top and especially the Hunter valley to a great new era. The Catskill Mountain Railroad had its trains meet the Hudson River Dayline at Catskill to transport summer vacationers to Lawrenceville, where they changed to the Otis Elevated Railroad for the Catskill Mountain House and other resorts in the area. The Ulster and Delaware Railroad brought passengers from Kingston to Phoenicia and then up through Stony Clove to Hunter, Tannersville and Haines Falls.

These railroads were a quick, easy, pleasant mode of travel from New York City to the growing resorts in the Catskills. John Ham of Hunter, an authority on the railroad era, has documents to show that as many as 26 trains passed through Haines Falls in a single day and that during some summers more than half a million people came to the Catskill Mountain resorts by train. This prosperous era, from about 1890 to 1930, ended with the Great Depression; the automobile also allowed people to travel more on their holidays rather than stay at one resort all summer long.

During this great summer resort era, exclusive private parks such as Onteora Park, Twilight Park, and Elka Park developed, with restricted member-ship favoring the wealthy and elite. Expensive summer homes also were built by wealthy city people such as the Colgate Family, the Macys and the Delafields.

Large hotels, such as the Catskill Mountain House, the Hotel Kaaterskill, the Laurel House and the Antlers, sprang up at Haines Falls. The Mansion House went up in Tannersville, and the Hunter House in Hunter along with many other large resorts. The Catskill Mountains became world-famous as a summer resort. The invigorating, fresh air, pure water and beauty of the mountains attracted people from far and wide. Guests at the Catskill Mountain House included former President Ulysses S. Grant and incumbent President Chester A. Arthur, among others. Windham valley, to a lesser extent, began to grow as a summer resort with places such as the Osborn House, the Thompson House and the Munson House.

The great influx of summer people from New York City and other cities created a great need for building supplies, workmen and farm produce. Big Hollow had them all, except the building supplies. The distance from Big Hollow to Tannersville is about eight miles, or less than a two-hour drive with a horse and buggy or on a bicycle, or even less time with a model-T Ford.

And so, the Hollow prospered with good times from 1890 to 1930. There was work for the carpenter, stonemason and gardener, also the waitress and cleaning lady. The farmer had a good market for his milk, cream, butter, eggs, poultry, maple syrup, garden products and wood fuel.

The population of Big Hollow at this time was around 200, with about half the people living in the village and the others on small farms that were self-sustaining. Here the wage-earner was employed part time and while at home maintained a good garden, cut his wood for fuel in the winter, kept a cow for milk and butter, a few hens for eggs and meat, and a couple of pigs to butcher in the fall for winter meat. He also had a horse to take him to and from work. It was a simple, good life with little income, few expenses, plenty of food, a warm home and a good family life.

OTHER OCCUPATIONS

Residents in the Hollow who had a career or trade were Mose Hitchcock, the local blacksmith; John Irish, shoe repairman; Archie and Richard Grey, upholsterers; Frank Palmer, wallpaper hanger, painter and barber; Raymond Moseman, school teacher; Gus Moseman, and later, Val Morrow, groceryman and postmaster; and John Phelps, operator of a sawmill behind his home for custom-sawing.

There were several chicken dealers in the village who supplied the big hotels and boarding houses in the Hunter Valley with chickens. These included Will Vining, Walter Bray, Gene Lewis and Ray Osborn. With model-T Ford trucks, they drove long distances to chicken farms, and then delivered chickens to a resort owner who would buy them to serve his guests. This business was hard work and required considerable traveling, but it was a lucrative summer occupation. In the autumn these men often would buy potatoes and in the spring purchase maple products from the local farmers to sell in Catskill and other Hudson Valley communities.

Also living in the Big Hollow village were a few retirees and widows and bachelors such as John Moseman, William Henry Moseman, Manley Mallory, Henry Vining, Charlie Hitchcock, Rose Hinman, Lydia Dubois, Charlotte Hitchcock and her widowed sister, Mary Frayer, and the two widowed sisters, Mrs. Zeal Rose and Mrs. Gus Lewis.

The Free Methodist parsonage was occupied over the years by many well remembered, deeply spiritual men and their families. Among those in this group were the Reverends W. G. Peterson, W.D. Lanning, L.H. Kelly, M.A. Parker, J.J. Gabriel, H.D. Olver, Jr., L.R. Guier and A.L. Payne. Their presence cast a spiritual influence not only over the members of their congregation, but over the entire valley as well, for they called at many homes and were concerned about the salvation of all people. Thus, the population of the little village was composed of a wide assortment of good people.

THE SUMMER RESORT BUSINESS

Shortly after the beginning of the present century, residents of New York City and New Jersey began coming to Big Hollow as summer guests. Spending their summer vacation with a farm family appealed to them. It was inspiring to observe family life at its best. The father, his wife and children all cooperated to do the work and survive as a rural, pioneer farm family. And the manifestation of this love, loyalty and togetherness afforded guests peace and contentment. Too, it was pleasant to hear a cow bell ringing in the pasture or hear a rooster crowing in the early morning hours. And walking around with the farmer as he did his chores—milking the cows, feeding the baby calves, driving the cows to pasture and harnessing the horses for their daily work—was interesting.

The farmhouse had its limitations. Although the bedrooms were immaculately clean, they were usually small, with no closets, indoor plumbing or electric lights. But the meals, served family-style, were delicious. There were creamy mashed potatoes, roast pork, beef or chicken served with gravy, and a great variety of vegetables fresh from the garden, topped off with home-made pie or cake and, on Sundays, home-made ice cream.

On the front porch, there was a row of rocking chairs. In the yard, one could find a hammock between two trees; a croquet court; a swing and more chairs under shady maple trees. There were many places to take walks—along the streams, through the woods, on the road or up one of the mountains. There were no "no trespassing" signs anywhere. And the mountain air was most invigorating.

At this time in our history, people desired vacations where they could relax, rest, and enjoy good food, without noise and excitement. The farm home with a nice, friendly family was the ideal place for such a vacation, at a cost of only five to fifteen dollars a week for room and three meals a day. The advent of the railroad and automobile made it easy to enjoy such a vacation in the Catskill Mountains.

Although many farm homes would take a few summer guests to supplement their income, there were several that accommodated as many as 15 to 25. One of the first of these large farm boarding houses was that of the George MacGlashan family, about a mile down from the end of the valley. A Pentecostal religious group from one of the churches in New York City began going to the MacGlashan home around 1920. They continued to come summers until 1980, when George's son and wife, Leon and Lillian, retired.

Another large farm boarding house was that of Jabez and Lizzie Barnum and their family. They had rooms for 15 to 20 guests. Newcomb and Grace Chatfield took a particular family and their friends for many summers. Mr. and Mrs. John VanLoan and son Harry and wife Mamie operated for many years a successful farm boarding resort on the Round Hill Road. And my grandmother, Emma Crandell, also filled her little house with four tiny bedrooms. Since she was a good cook she usually had her house full with other guests taking rooms in neighboring homes who came in for meals.

As the years went by and the deer population increased in the mountains, hunters began coming to the Catskills in late autumn. Iris and Wilfred Hitchcock and Lillian and Leon MacGlashan took visiting hunters for many years and made many friends with these fine people.

THE SUGAR MAPLES RESORT

On April 20, 1883, Sherwood A. "Gus" Moseman was born in Big Hollow to Jennie and Robert Moseman. This baby was destined to have a momentous influence on Big Hollow, an influence which would make a lasting change in the way of life in the little hamlet. Gus grew to be a remarkable, versatile man. He was tall, handsome and intelligent, with a heavy resonant voice which commanded respect. He had a winning personality, was friendly, and somewhat aloof.

Gus was a master and leader in many ways. He was a musician with a strong baritone voice, a skilled pianist, and the director of the choir in the Presbyterian Church for a long time. He was a better-than-average artist with watercolors. He was a tailor, and at one time made dresses for his three daughters when they were in elementary school. When it came to business, Mr. Moseman was visionary, adventuresome and prudent.

Early in life, Gus's father, Robert, died and his mother sometime later married her brother-in-law, William Henry Moseman. For many years, William Henry operated the local grocery store and served as Big Hollow postmaster. Gus worked in the store and went to the one-room school below the village. Later, he attended Albany Business College.

As a young man, Gus married Adelaide (Addie) Newkirk of Hensonville and they had three daughters—Fredonia, Bertha and Vernette. All the girls were as musical as their father.

For several years, Mr. Moseman helped his step-father to enlarge and improve the Big Hollow store. Later, he moved to Staten Island and opened a mercantile business there, which in a few short years became one of the largest of its kind on Staten Island. Feeling called to serve his country in W.W. I, he sold his business to enlist in the service. When the war ended, he returned with his family to Big Hollow and took over the store and post office again.

While in Staten Island, Mr. Moseman had made contact with wholesale businesses in New York City and upon his return to Big Hollow, he began another venture. He purchased from discount houses and salesrooms in New York City clothing, shoes, ornaments, decorations and odds and ends which would appeal to farming people. These were displayed at reasonable prices in his Big Hollow Store. A big publicity campaign was launched. Nearly every housewife in the village was hired as a clerk and on the mornings of the two-day sales, the street would be lined with cars from far and near as people drove long distances to ''snap up'' bargains at the opening of the doors.

Upon his return to Big Hollow, Mr. Moseman purchased the old house east of the Methodist Church, which he enlarged and renovated into a beautiful home. As time went on, friends of the Moseman family from Staten Island and the City came to Big Hollow to visit the Mosemans and remained for a week or two. As more came, new and larger facilities were necessary to entertain them.

In 1925, Mr. Moseman sold the store and gave up the post office to Valentine W. Morrow, an enterprising young man who would serve the community for 40 years as merchant and postmaster. Mr. Moseman borrowed $75,000 from Charles Phelps, a boyhood schoolmate who had become a prosperous lumber dealer in Cairo and Windham. A large dining room with a capacity for seating 650 people was built as was another building for office space, recreation and bedrooms. As the years passed and more rooms were needed, half of the houses in the village, a total of eight, were acquired and eight large two-story motels were erected, enabling the resort to accommodate more than 500 guests.

Mr. Moseman knew how to entertain summer visitors. His charming personality and the beautiful luxurious facilities of the resort appealed to guests who desired a restful and enjoyable vacation. The dining room was attractive and the food was delicious. College girls served as waitresses.

For entertainment, there were guided hikes, horseback riding, bicycling, tennis courts, a baseball field with roofed bleachers, a huge heated outdoor swimming pool with raised bleachers, a roller-skating rink, a real Indian who lived in his own tepee on the grounds, a large black bear in his wire cage, a library and an orchestra for dining and dancing. The grounds were spacious and beautiful with evergreen trees, shrubbery, many flowers and delightful paths and benches.

In particular, there were a good number of sugar maples, which also lined the town's streets and dotted its mountains. And in 1921, the name Big Hollow was changed to Maplecrest, with the resort adopting the name of Sugar Maples.

Mr. Moseman was the general manager of Sugar Maples. John Martin, a long time friend of the Mosemans, was superintendent of maintenance and personnel, supervising some 110 employees. Mrs. Moseman and daughters supervised the work in the huge kitchen and coffee shop.

During the four summer months, there was a large change of summer guests every two weeks. Many drove their cars from New York City. Others came on the Hudson River Dayline or on the train to Catskill where they were met by large seven-passenger limousines from the Sugar Maples which would transport them to the large resort within the hour.

The Sugar Maples Hotel greatly transformed the life of the community during the four summer months. Mr. Moseman and Mr. Martin operated it from about 1925 to 1960. Employment was given to many local people. Rooms were rented in local homes for the excess registration at the Hotel. There was a great demand for dairy products, poultry, fruit and vegetables and other foods, equipment and merchandise. No alcoholic beverages were ever sold on the premises. Guests were encouraged to attend local church services. There was an atmosphere of culture and refinement at Sugar Maples. The great influx of guests so increased the population of the village that the sidewalk was unable to accommodate all of the people at mealtime so the village street became the sidewalk. The natives either slowly followed behind in their cars or gently nudged their way through the group.

Now, in 1993, the village has greatly changed since 1925. Many houses are empty. There is only one church. There is no longer a blacksmith shop or garage or store. The little village gives the appearance of a ghost town.

The little community, as it approaches its 200th birthday in 1995, has passed from a colonial settlement and development of small farms and a few industries including the resort business, to more or less a quiet, residential community, with many new homes of city dwellers who live only part of the time in the valley.

THE FARMER'S LIFE

In THE first part of the twentieth century, life was simple and good in Big Hollow. Neighbors were friendly and helpful. Pa could call Mr. Planck night or day and say, "I have a sick cow, Jake, could you come down?" And since all travel was either on foot or in a horse-drawn wagon, travelers were pleased at the opportunity to stop and chat for a few minutes.

Through the winter months, there occasionally would be a church or Boy Scout supper in some large farmhouse to raise funds. The men would gather together in a large room to smoke, discuss their work, recall the old days, or talk about fox hunting. The women would be in the kitchen getting the food, usually a chicken and biscuit dinner, ready to serve on the long dining room table. A bedroom would be set up where the young people could play kissing games, such as "Four Old Maids," "Shoo-Fly," or "Hi Jim Along." When the evening was over, the men would get the horses and hitch them to the wagon or sleigh to return home. Everyone was tired and in a hurry to go home and to bed with pleasant thoughts about good food, good conversation and good neighbors.

In the farm home, everyone worked. The girls helped the mother with the household chores and caring for the younger children. The boys helped with the farm chores, filled the wood box and did odd jobs on the farm.

There was little sickness and few accidents, but the mother was knowledgeable about colds, sore throat, constipation, bruises and upset stomachs. Her medicine cabinet was filled with such things as castor oil, syrup of figs, malena pills, Lee's Save the Baby, cough syrup and Watkins salves. For croup or a chest cold, she would make a flaxseed or skunk oil poultice. Cow manure poultices were also used.

Most families lived in the large kitchen which contained the cooking range, dining table, kitchen sink, possibly an old sofa and a variety of chairs. It was the only room kept warm in the winter. After the day's work was done and the supper dishes were washed and put away, the family would gather about the table with one large lamp in the center of the table. The mother would patch clothes or mend socks while the father would read a farm paper and the children would do their homework. Sometimes, apples or popcorn would add to the family's enjoyment, as they discussed the events of the day or plans for the future. The family, being close together and visiting with one another in the home, built a strong and loving relationship which lasted through life.

At around eight or nine o'clock, it was time for bed and there would be a rush through the cold hall with a hot flat iron or soap stone to the bedrooms, where prayers would be said and sleep would come quickly and peacefully.

The farmers in the Hollow had a good life and did well during these years, 1915-1925, even though they worked hard. Their work was pleasant—being outdoors close to nature and caring for domestic animals. Farm work is a great blessing. At this time there were few tensions or pressures associated with it. Little was known of the outside world. A few farmers subscribed to the *Windham Journal* and maybe one farm paper such as the *American Agriculturist.* There were no radios, televisions, moving pictures, and only local telephones. Attention and minds were nearly entirely devoted to home life and work.

A farmer's monetary income was a trifle, but he had few expenses. The monthly milk check from the creamery was the most constant and dependable source of revenue. Then, there would be additional income from the sale of firewood, maple syrup and sugar, or livestock for meat and breeding purposes.

Each morning, the farmer would take his milk to the local milk station with his horse and wagon where it would be weighed, tested for butter fat and separated. The skimmed milk, he could take back home at no cost to feed to his calves, chickens and pigs. Unfortunately the creamery check was usually used up almost entirely to pay for grain for the livestock and groceries for the family. Taxes in those days were very reasonable.

Since wood was the only fuel used in the early 1900's, there was a great demand for it by most schools, churches, businesses and private homes. My father sometimes would have as many as 50 cords of wood to sell, at five dollars a cord, delivered to Windham.

Our big wood lot was three miles away from home on the side of Windham High Peak. Saturdays Pa and I would drive up there, cut as many poles and logs as we could, and during the next week, while I was in school, he would draw them down home to be sawed, split, and piled. About 20 cords were to be used in our home and the rest was sold at Hensonville and Windham. During the winter months, much wood was also cut by strong powerful men like the DeLong boys—Merritt, Vernon and Calvin—and John Oliver and his sons—Clarence, Emory and Wiltsey—and others like them. These woodcutters could cut a tree with a cross-cut saw into 16 inch lengths, split the blocks into slabs, and pile them for one dollar a cord. They could cut, split and pile eight to ten cords a day. On one occasion, Calvin DeLong and John Winchell cut 26 cords of wood in a single day for Jacob Planck!

Another winter occupation for the farmer was filling his ice house to cool his milk during the summer months. When the ice reached a thickness of 12 to 14 inches on the creek or on the farmer's private pond, it was marked out, cut with a hand saw, and hauled to the ice house where it was packed in sawdust. The next summer the ice would be used to cool the milk in a vat, occasionally make a freezer of ice cream, or be sold at twenty five cents a cake to village dwellers who had an ice box. Some housewives kept perishable foods fresh in a cool, damp cellar with an earthen floor, and others would lower foods in a pail down into the well just above the water.

Early in the spring, about mid-March, the farmer would notice that the days were getting longer and the sun was shining brighter. The maple syrup season was arriving. First the buckets were scattered through the maple sugar bush where the trees later would be tapped and the buckets attached to a spile to gather the sap. The sap then would be boiled into syrup either in a hog's head or an evaporator. About 30 to 40 gallons of sap were required to make one gallon of syrup. When the season was well under way, residents in the valley could look up along the side of the mountain and observe the steam from various sap houses rising up above the trees.

The pure, golden maple syrup at one time sold for as little as one dollar a gallon, but over the years the price increased until now, in 1993, it is selling for twenty-five dollars a gallon. Other products of the maple industry were hard maple sugar in cakes and maple butter. The good housewife in the home usually boiled the syrup to a greater density and then stirred this syrup into either hard sugar or maple butter.

After the maple syrup season ended about the middle of April, the buckets and other utensils were gathered, washed and stored away in the house or barn for another year.

By this time the farmer would begin thinking of the planting season and getting his equipment ready for planting the crops, including the garden, and harvesting hay later in the summer. In early colonial days, harvesting hay with hand tools and crude machinery was a big job. The fields were often rough and stony. Much of the hay was mowed with a scythe and collected with a hand rake. Iron-wheeled mowing machines mowed the smoother fields, and high-wheeled iron rakes, horse-drawn, made windrows, which were later made into heaps with a pitch fork. Then the farmer with his son or hired man and a high iron-tired wagon and hay rigging would go around the field gathering the hay. One man would pitch the hay onto the wagon with his fork while the other would load it, stomp it down, and drive the team. This continued until a high load of hay was on the wagon which was then drawn to the barn, pitched off, and stowed away, all by hand. Haying sometimes lasted until the middle of September. The horse-drawn hay fork for pulling hay up into the roof of the barn and then dropping it into the hay mow didn't come into the Hollow until the late 1920's. Haying was a back-breaking, exhausting, dirty and sweaty job in the summer months.

Several farmers in the Valley purchased silos in the 1920's for storing silage corn. The first farmers to have silos were Newell Peck, Jacob Planck, Ros Vining, and Will Hitchcock. The field corn became ready to harvest about the middle of September, usually before the frost hit it. Corn harvesting was also back-breaking work. The rows of tall stalks were cut close to the ground with a hand sickle and placed in little bundles. Several men would work at this job at a time. These bundles of corn would later be lifted onto a wagon with a hay rigging and drawn to the silo where it was run through an ensilage cutter and blown in short lengths to the top of the silo where it would fall down into the silo. Then it would be stomped down and allowed to settle for a day or two. Filling the silo would then start again until it was full. Corn silage was excellent winter feed for dairy cows and young cattle, a good supplement to hay and grain.

Farmers, with their teams of horses, drew stone from stone walls, meadows and pastures and even along the highway to the stone crusher, where it was broken up and then drawn to the road where it was to be used. Here men with sledge hammers would break the crushed stone even smaller, level it off and pound it into the ground. The steam roller would then smooth the road, after which finer crushed stone and stone dust would be spread and rolled into the road to make a smooth, hard surface.

Many men were needed to load the wagons with stone, feed the crusher, and pound the stone into the road. The going wage for many years for these laborers was forty cents an hour. Local farmers with their teams of horses would draw the stone from the field to the crusher and then draw the crushed stone from the crusher bins to where the road was being built. This routine would be followed all day long. The money paid the farmer for the use of his team, wagon, and his own work was six dollars a day.

Politics often played a part in local road building. One autumn my father heard that the town was planning to build a section of road from Hensonville to Maplecrest. We had lumber sawed for a new wagon box so we would be ready when the work began. But we weren't called to report. It so happened on a Monday morning around 7:30 we looked out of our kitchen window and saw our neighbor, Mr. Jacob Planck, with his big black team and wagon drive by, followed closely by his son John with his team and wagon. Unfortunately for us, my father was a Republican. Mr. Planck and John were Democrats. And the Superintendent of Highways and the Town Board at that time were members of the Democratic Party. Pa wasn't given any work that year on the town highway.

SPECIAL PEOPLE OF BIG HOLLOW

RAY OSBORN

RAY Osborn was the only child of Frankie and Henry Osborn. The Osborns lived in the little house east of the original Free Methodist Church where Walter Baker now lives. Henry kept a couple of cows and had a good garden. Frankie was one of the founders and a pillar in the Free Methodist Church. Ray was energetic, enthusiastic and bubbled over with life. He was a great-great-grandson of Deacon Lemuel Hitchcock.

As a young man, Ray and his friend, Merritt DeLong on Barnum Hill, enjoyed going to parties with nice carriage horses and rubber-tired wagons. They also hunted foxes together and were good friends for many years. For some time each had his own model-T touring car in which they raced around taking girls to picnics and other social events.

In the coming years, Ray married Zada Brandow, a beautiful girl from Prattsville. They acquired the home in the village where Ray's grandfather Lem Hitchcock and Sarah had lived. Soon Ray had a pick-up truck with which he was drawing wood and buying and selling calves. Later, he started a small dairy in the old barn, bought more land, and eventually had a milking dairy of 30 to 40 cows. At the same time, he began speculating in cattle and built up a large cattle business.

When a valley farm became abandoned, Ray would buy it, and arrange for Roy MacGlashan to move his sawmill to the farm. He would cut the logs on the woodlot, sell some of the lumber and use part of it to rebuild the house and barn into modern buildings. Then, at a later date, he would sell the farm at a profit. At one time or another, he purchased, improved and sold the George Drum, Zalmon Hitchcock and Billy Crandell farms.

Along with the operation of the dairy farm, and speculating in the cattle business, Ray managed during the different seasons of the year to buy and sell maple sugar and syrup, and potatoes from the local farms. When the opportunity developed to provide transportation for Sugar Maples' guests from the Catskill

River Dayline on the Hudson and the railroad to the Sugar Maples Resort, Ray was quick to secure large seven-passenger limousines and buses and take on this additional lucrative business.

Baseball was ingrained in the hearts of the men and boys in Big Hollow, and Ray was a born baseball player. He was an exceptional player in any position and was full of spirit and enthusiasm for the game. Although there were no young men his age in the Hollow at that time who played ball, he managed to get together a team of older men like my father and us boys. Soon, we were playing games with neighboring teams such as Ashland, Prattsville, Lanesville and East Jewett. Ray provided the players with good bats, a catcher's outfit, a few gloves and new balls. And with Ray as our leader and coach we won games.

One summer, I played outfield and Pa, first base. When he batted, I stood by the plate and ran the bases for him. Reg Bennett of Chichester was a dynamic player with a hot temper. He and Ray would almost get into a fight over an umpire's questionable decision. Dave Robinson of East Jewett was a speed-ball pitcher with poor control, and East Jewett usually beat us. But we were a good team.

As time went on, baseball became more popular in the Hollow, and we began playing "out of our class" teams. Sugar Maples was growing rapidly with summer guests who enjoyed watching a good ball game. The resort constructed a beautiful field at the rear of their buildings with a roofed grandstand. It was a beautiful location—watching a game, sitting in lounge chairs and enjoying the panoramic beauty of the mountains and sky.

Preston Hollow had a strong team with the Dingman brothers, George Edwards and several other skilled players. I don't recall ever winning a game against them. Once when I was pitching and doing remarkably well, we kept ahead of them for several innings. For some reason they just couldn't seem to get many hits on this particular day. When we were several runs ahead, I decided to take it a little easy and let some of the fielders do more of the work. It was a foolish mistake. Preston Hollow began hitting and scoring runs. When I tried to stop them by pitching with everything I had, they continued to hit. Finally, I was replaced on the mound and Preston Hollow won the game. It was a good lesson for me to do my best at all times and to never let up.

It was during the 1930's that our team was at its best. We were playing every Saturday afternoon during the summer months and spectators were coming from long distances to enjoy the games. Sugar Maples and the other summer resorts in the area were filled to capacity with New York City guests.

We had heard about the House of David, a traveling baseball team, which played in the smaller cities and large communities. The team was made up, probably, of college students who liked to play ball during the summer months and also earn some money. The players were fine young men, slim, with dark beards, and a few of them were Jewish and Black. To arrange for this rather well-known team to come to Big Hollow required a guarantee to them of a sizeable honorarium, but we did it.

The game with the House of David drew a capacity crowd. They were not only a good team, but they were pleasant, agreeable and friendly. They never protested an umpire's decision. Between innings, they would often entertain the spectators with clever passing of the ball or other antics.

During the game, we were allowed to make a fairly good showing by hitting some long drives, stealing bases and scoring a few runs; while our opponents appeared to be playing at their best, even to the extent of showing despair over the way the game was going.

In the several games we played with the House of David over two or three summers, our team usually could keep ahead by a run or two, or at least keep the score even until about the eighth inning, when it just seemed that we began to play poorly and, by luck, the House of David seemed to improve and would win the game by only a run or two. But they always won!

It was during these years when our team was at its best and Sugar Maples was at its peak of prosperity and development that something was happening to our team that would soon destroy it. As we played better teams, we began importing better players from Kingston, Oneonta and smaller neighboring communities. These players replaced our local boys. I soon found myself only playing part of a game occasionally. I remember one afternoon not even going to the game, but staying home and painting the barn, even though Pa was an avid fan and went to the game. As fewer local boys played, interest and the spirit of the team seemed to die, and in the next few years the team went out of existence, never to be revived.

During my lifetime, I played ball for many years—on the high school team and at college—and I attended many games as a spectator. But I never had the joy of playing baseball as I did those games with the House of David on the Sugar Maples field.

By now, Ray was growing older and his interest in baseball was being replaced with his family and business activities. His four children, Evelyn, Geraldine, Beatrice and Buddy, were grown and attending school or helping with the business.

Ray had now become a local John Deere farm machinery dealer, and although there were fewer farms in the Windham area, there were large farms in Delaware County and large contractors provided a market for John Deere tractors and other equipment. Ray soon had a thriving, prosperous dealership.

Once a year, his company sponsored a ''John Deere day'' at Ray's place of business. New tractors were exhibited, moving pictures shown, company representatives were on hand to answer questions and quantities of delicious food were served. John Deere Day was a big day for Ray and his family and for

Maplecrest. It drew more people than Moseman's store sales had more than two decades earlier.

Ray was a versatile man. He was a good businessman, great promoter and good man for his community. He and his family attended and supported the Free Methodist Church. He made Maplecrest a popular baseball center. He employed local men. He was generous and supported good causes. Ray brought new and fresh life to Maplecrest and was an inspiration to all who knew him.

VALENTINE W. MORROW

Around 1915, Val Morrow came to Big Hollow as a summer guest from New York City with young friends, Tom Rogers, George Tolman and a Mr. and Mrs. Keller. The first summer they boarded at the farm home of Anson Hitchcock on the Slater Road, and later for several years at the little farm home of Emma and Billy Crandell, which was across the bridge on the Slater Road.

Val and his friends loved nature, the mountains and hiking. They made regular hikes over the Ridge Road and on to Silver Lake, a good five miles each way and also climbed several mountains such as Windham High Peak and Black Head.

From 1917 until 1919, Val was in active service in World War I in France. During the War, his hearing was impaired, which allowed him to draw a small pension for the rest of his life. While coming to Big Hollow, Val met a charming young local girl by the name of Irene Mallory. They were married in 1918, and during the years which followed had a daughter Lorna and son Elwood. This happy marriage lasted for nearly 67 years. Returning from military service, Val did odd jobs on the mountain top. For several summers, he and Irene operated the concession stand at Silver Lake for the owner, a Mr. St. Johns. For a short time he worked for the Jewett town highway department and also wired several homes with electricity after the power line came to the mountains in the early 1920's.

It was about this time that Val and Irene purchased the large house later occupied by the John West family in East Jewett, and began taking summer guests.

Val Morrow was a good, Christian man—industrious, intelligent and public-spirited. He was thoughtful, soft-spoken and a man of few words. But he exerted a powerful influence on Big Hollow (Maplecrest in 1926) and the mountain top area.

In 1925, when Mr. Moseman was starting Sugar Maples, he sold the grocery store to Val and Irene, and Val received the appointment as postmaster. For 40 years, from 1925 to 1965, Val and Irene operated the Maplecrest store and post office. Val was more than a courteous, dependable postmaster; he became an authority on postal rules and regulations and attended state and national conventions of postmasters. In the store, Irene excelled as a manager and clerk. She knew the Maplecrest people and loved them. Calling at the store for groceries and the mail gave one a cheerful uplift. The store and post office over the years also gave a great boost to Sugar Maples, as Val and Irene became acquainted with the guests and welcomed many back each year. The store and post office also helped to develop a strong, united community spirit.

When the WAJ centralized school district was established in the early 1930's, Val became one of the first five schoolboard members representing the Maplecrest and East Jewett areas. For many years he served faithfully and well, helping to construct a large new building, establishing new departments and curricula, and setting up bus routes.

Shortly after coming to Maplecrest, Val became a member of the Mountain Lodge, Free And Accepted Masons, and later served as its Master. He became High Priest of the Council and Representative of the Grand Lodge of New Jersey F. & A.M.

Realizing the importance and value of a public library in promoting the educational and cultural life of the area, Val gave hours of his time to the work and meetings of the Windham Public Library as a trustee. He was a past commander of Sgt. James F. Carty D.S.C. Post 1545, Veterans of Foreign Wars, and a member of Mohican Post 983 of the American Legion. Val was also one of the founding members of the Batavia Kill Watershed District and the C.D. Lane Lake and Recreational Park. The park pavilion building is named in his honor.

It is only natural that, since Val loved the outdoors and had been a boy scout in the city, he wanted other boys to share the benefits of the scouting program. He started an active troop in Maplecrest that continued for many years. Also, with Rev. Wells of Windham, he helped get scouting started in other communities. At one time, there were strong, active troops at Windham, Ashland, Prattsville, Lexington and Tannersville. It was during these years that Val became a member of the Rip Van Winkle Boy Scout Council, which served Greene and Ulster Counties, with headquarters in Kingston. He journeyed to Kingston to the monthly meetings and had a major role in helping to develop the Council's Camp Tri-Mount at East Jewett with its large dining hall, lake and several hundred acres of mountain land. The East Jewett Troop, which was an outgrowth of the Maplecrest Troop, trained six scouts to rise to the highest rank in scouting—that of Eagle Scout. Val's enthusiasm, hard work and leadership in the Boy Scouts benefited many boys and men over the years on the mountaintop and in Greene and Ulster Counties.

The Maplecrest United Methodist Church grew and thrived under Val and Irene's dedicated work and leadership. A large dining room and kitchen were added to the church. The sanctuary interior was redecorated. New oak pews, made by Edward MacGlashan of Chestertown, were installed. A new electronic organ was given to the church by Sterling Planck. There were dinners, fairs and rummage sales conducted by the ladies of the church. Val served as trustee, treasurer and secretary. He was also the Sunday school superintendent and adult class teacher. Irene, too, was a strong worker and leader in the Ladies Aid and the Sunday school. Summer Sunday night services were very popular and were attended by the waitresses from the resort hotels and also the summer guests.

During the years 1956 to 1972, the Rev. Merton S. Cady and family served the Hensonville Charge. These were the golden years for the Charge and the three churches of Hensonville, Maplecrest and East Jewett. Each summer, there was daily vacation Bible school for the children. There were Holy Week services, an active Methodist Men's Club and a strong spirit of love, cooperation and good will among the three churches of the Charge. Val represented the Maplecrest Church on the Hensonville Charge Committee during these years.

On March 15, 1983, at 86, Val Morrow died in his home in Maplecrest. He was a good man who'd lived a long, happy and useful life.

JACOB D. PLANCK

Mr. Planck bought the old farm on the hill above our farm in 1878. It was an old run-down farm with unworked fields of brush and weeds, and old weather-beaten buildings. Mr. Planck was a young man, newly married to Ella Miles of Jewett. He was desperately poor, unable to read or write, but an industrious man with boundless enthusiasm and vision. He was to become a good friend, a helpful neighbor and an influential man in the community.

Soon, with borrowed money and inexhaustible energy, Mr. Planck made the old farm look better. Fences were repaired, a small dairy appeared, fields were plowed and fertilized. A crowing rooster awakened a small flock of laying hens every morning. A ditch was dug to a flowing spring on the mountain-side. Hemlock pipe logs were laid and a big stream of pure mountain water began filling a tub at the barn for the cows and horses. The overflow from that tub ran to another big tub outside the kitchen door and the overflow pipe logs from the second tub ran to a third one by the road on the hill for traveling horses to drink. For this, the town paid Mr. Planck an annual stipend.

At the end of 20 years, the farm was paid for. Buildings were repaired, painted, and in excellent condition. The fields were productive, and in the pastures was a herd of young, healthy milking cows. The farm had become a profitable, attractive business.

Mr. Planck was a man of medium size—thin, rather tall, with a beard and sideburns. He was confident—somewhat aggressive, with quite definite convictions. Yet he had a sense of humor and smiled and chuckled easily. He spoke with authority, and although others might disagree with him, they seldom, if ever, argued with him. Although there were 50 years' difference in our ages, I liked and admired Mr. Planck as a neighbor and friend.

He told me once when he was driving by our place with his horse and buggy that he saw me going from the house to the barn with my mother's big butcher knife. When he inquired where I was going with the knife, I replied, "to butcher the bull.'' My uncle, Dwight, who lived next door, was a butcher and even though I was only four or five years old, I occasionally strolled down to the slaughter house to watch him butcher a cow, sheep or pig. Mr. Planck laughed about my remark.

Mr. Planck's son, Maurice, and his wife Ethel lived in a tenant house on an estate at St. Remy, near Kingston. Maurice was foreman of the farm and superintendent of the grounds. Once a year, Mr. Planck would hire Robert Peck to drive his car to Kingston for an overnight visit with Maurice and Ethel. Several times when I was around 10 or 12 years old, Mr. Planck invited me to go with him to visit Maurice. To me, at that time, it was like a present-day trip to London or Paris. I would sit in the back seat alone, enjoying the scenery and hearing Mr. Planck and Robert visit. At Maurice's, it was pleasant to walk around the farm and listen to Mr. Planck chat with Maurice and Ethel. I greatly appreciated Mr. Planck's kindness in taking me on those trips with him.

Mr. Planck was a proud man. He strove to be first and have the best. His horses were the biggest and best team in the valley. Nearly all the farmers had a conventional three-by-eight foot evaporator for boiling maple sap, but Mr. Planck had a much larger one—a four-by-ten foot, which provided 16 more square feet of pan space over the fire in the arch, enabling him to boil the same amount of sap in much less time.

When automobiles came around in the early 1900's, Mr. Planck, although he never learned to drive a car, purchased an Overland touring car which was in a class above a Model-T Ford or Chevrolet. Some years later when enclosed cars appeared, Mr. Planck was one of the first to buy a new Chevrolet four-door sedan with disk wheels and flower vases on the posts between the front and rear doors. He kept his cars spotlessly clean and covered with a dust cloth in the barn.

He was one of the first farmers to have a silo for storing corn ensilage. We had a silo, too, with a six horsepower engine to cut the corn and blow it through a pipe to the top of the silo where it fell inside. The engine wasn't powerful enough to always blow the cut corn up the silo pipe which often would clog. Mr. Planck didn't have this problem, for his engine was twice the size of ours.

Mr. and Mrs. Planck were religious people. They were faithful in their attendance and support of the Methodist Church. Over the years, however, I heard rumors about Mr. Planck which disturbed me. My uncle, Roswell Vining, had worked for him as a poor, young boy and on one occasion when the Plancks were entertaining friends for noon dinner, they hadn't called Uncle Ros, and as a result he worked all day long picking up stones without any dinner. Another story I recall is that when my grandfather, Billy Crandell, was janitor of the Methodist Church, it was agreed he was to receive the church offering, which usually amounted to less than a dollar, for his services. One Sunday, my grandmother noticed a dollar bill in the collection plate which was not turned over to my grandfather. Going up to Mr. Planck's early Monday morning, my grandfather said, ''Jake, I want that dollar bill.'' Without hesitation or comment, Mr. Planck gave him the dollar!

During the summer months, the farmers sold their milk in 40-quart cans to milk dealers who supplied the big boarding houses in the Tannersville area. The dairymen were paid on the basis of the measured quart, without consideration for the butter fat content of the milk. A dealer happened to catch Mr. Planck rinsing his milking pails and pouring the rinsing water into the milk can with the milk he was paid for.

As I grew older, I wondered if Mr. Planck had a happy home life. Mrs. Planck never went with him to St. Remy to visit their son. In fact, I never saw them together anywhere. The two sons were seldom seen at their parents' home or with them. The boys would refer to their father as ''the old man,'' and often chuckled over the things he said and did.

When Harold Dougherty, the Plancks' hired man, was seriously wounded by a shot from Albert Bray's rifle while they were target practicing up in the woods, Dr. Sidney Ford, the local family doctor reported that there was no hope of Harold's living. The bullet had entered his right arm, passed through it and his body, narrowly missing his heart, and had lodged in his left arm. Harold continued to live and was in the Plancks' home for several days. Meanwhile, Mrs. Planck prayed that he repent and become a Christian and that his life be spared. Harold became a Christian. It was generally believed it was Mrs. Planck's prayers for him that saved his life and soul. Many, many years later, Harold suddenly died while working for Ted Smith, of Ashland, as a farm hand.

In his late 60's, Mr. Planck became totally blind. The day he returned from the hospital, I sat at the end of our front walk watching for him. Toward night, I saw his car coming up the road. He sat tall and straight, with his head up. He didn't look at me or wave. I sobbed as I walked back toward the house and Mother. I knew my friend would never see me again.

Soon, he disposed of his farm possessions and became house-bound—listening to his little Crosley, battery-operated radio with its head phones. I walked up the hill one evening a week to sit with him. He enjoyed reporting to me the current news of the day. One night I was sadly shocked when he mentioned he had seen the price of milk was going up. Mrs. Planck burst out laughing, loudly exclaiming, ''What do you mean, 'You seen'? Why, you are blind as a bat!'' In his early 70's, he told me one evening he would give everything he owned, even his clothes, if he could have his eyesight back. Aside from this, however, I never heard him complain once about his blindness.

I still have the two gold pieces he gave me for my high school graduation. Somehow, Mr. Planck made me feel I was special to him and that he needed me. I always respected and admired him for being so strong and confident, although he was illiterate and had to sign his name with an ''x'', followed by Mrs. Planck's signature.

Mr. Planck died at his home in June, 1933. It so happened that his funeral was on the day of my graduation from the New Paltz Normal School. It presented a problem to my parents as to where to go. The Plancks and our family had been next door neighbors for over fifty years without ever having a single dispute. Pa went up to the Planck sons to ask for their suggestions. One of them nonchalantly replied, ''Why, go to the graduation by all means. The old man wouldn't care.''

MORE PEOPLE OF BIG HOLLOW

WILLIAM PHELPS

A LITTLE spring bubbles up from the ground in the basin at the far end of the valley. It is the source of the Batavia Kill creek, which flows westward for 20 miles through the Windham Valley and Ashland Valley, then joins the Schoharie Creek from the Hunter Valley just east of Prattsville Village. Together, these two streams flow into Gilboa Reservoir about two miles west of Prattsville.

The spring, at one time, had been surrounded by tall virgin pine, hemlock and spruce trees. In the early days of the settlement, the trees had been cut and the land cleared below the spring. On the north side of the stream, a house and farm buildings had been erected for a farm. One of the first known settlers on this farm was William Phelps, a farmer and lumber man. A dam was built across the little stream and a water-wheel provided power for the mill.

At this mill, long, wide, first-quality boards were sawed as well as strong planks and two-by-fours to be delivered by teams of horses and oxen to distant lumberyards. Little is known of William Phelps, except that he was a good businessman and wise lumberman. Will had three wives. The second one had a son by her first husband. This young man was well known for his great strength. He traveled for some time with a circus demonstrating his strength. A leather harness over his shoulders enabled him to use his whole body in lifting unbelievable weights. One occasion when his step-father's steam engine had become stuck in mud, several teams of horses were unable to move the big machine. Finally, the stout man lifted a wheel at a time from the mud, held it until blocks were placed underneath, and the horses pulled the big engine to its destination. He was known as the ''Samson of Big Hollow.'' William and his third wife had a son by the name of John, who grew up to make lumbering a career. John married Emma Seeley and they became the parents of Charles Phelps and Mildred Phelps, who later married Earl Ostrander. They had a daughter Althea, who died young, and a son, Earl Jr. (Ozzie), who saw action in World War II and later became a well-known, prosperous car salesman. Charles Phelps established a prosperous lumber business with yards in Catskill, Cairo and Windham, and a mill in the Adirondacks at Chestertown. Charles and his wife, Inez Mallory, and their daughter Arbreta were dedicated Christian people. Although they lived in Cairo, they were faithful members of the Maplecrest Free Methodist Church. All three were generous, giving thousands of dollars to churches and charitable organizations.

Many years after the lumber had been cut in the basin at the end of the Hollow and the dam had filled up with silt, Dr. Alfred Gundersen purchased the Phelps property in 1919 as a summer home. Dr. Gundersen was a native of Norway. He was a distinguished-looking man with a beard and a high squeaky voice. He was quiet, retiring and humble, and appeared almost timid. He was a botanist, educated at Stanford, Harvard and the Sorbonne in Paris. Dr. Gundersen was curator at the Brooklyn Botanic Garden for 30 years. He was married and had two daughters, Sylvia and Ellen.

Dr. Gundersen loved this remote, old farmhouse at the end of the valley surrounded by mountains and with a beautiful view to the west. For years he escaped the noisy city on weekends by taking a train or a boat to Catskill and then hiking over the mountains from Acra to his lonely mountain home. His family spent the summers there.

Christianity and education were very important to Dr. and Mrs. Gundersen, and they wanted their daughters to have a good basic foundation in both. Saugerties, a small village on the west bank of the Hudson River between New York and Big Hollow, had a superior public school under the leadership of Dr. Grant D. Morse, the Superintendent of Schools. In 1927, Dr. Gundersen purchased a home in Saugerties where Sylvia and Ellen might attend this excellent school situated in a rural area with the beautiful Catskill Mountains to the west. This became the Gundersen's winter home and Mr. Gundersen commuted from the city to be with his family on weekends. The family stayed at their Big Hollow home during the two summer months.

For the girls' spiritual training, their father brought them to the Big Hollow Presbyterian Church and Sunday school. At that time, there were about 20 in the congregation—most of them members of the Platt Hitchcock family. The girls began Sunday school in my mother's or Aunt Julia Vining's class and then when they became older they were moved up to the Young People's Class taught by Aunt Mary Frier.

Dr. Gundersen went into Uncle Zal Hitchcock's Men's Class with my father and Uncle Ros Vining. The teaching and class discussions must have been dull and elementary to Dr. Gundersen, as the teacher and the other two class members had probably had only a few years of schooling. But Dr. Gundersen was a perfect class member, giving full attention, reading when asked to, answering questions, and showing the utmost respect to his teacher and fellow class members.

One summer, he suggested that the class study other religions of the world. I recall that an attempt was made, but since the teacher had no preparation and the other class members showed little interest, the class was soon back to reading and discussing the lessons of the Bible.

As this intelligent, highly educated gentleman sat in the Sunday school class week after week with three simple, poorly educated farmers, he must have been impressed with their strong faith in God. These men, their wives and children were always at church on Sunday. God and the church had top priority in their lives. Their faith and dedication touched Dr. Gundersen's heart. His daughters and their families became devout Christians.

Having been brought up and educated in an atmosphere of culture and refinement, Dr. Gundersen was always careful to look his best. Shortly after coming to Big Hollow, I saw him one day going toward the village on his bicycle. He dismounted just east of the village at a small clump of trees, put on his necktie, combed his hair and smoothed his coat. Then he continued on his way to the local store and post office. I have always remembered this little incident as at that time men wore neckties only on special occasions and clothes were changed only once a week for washing.

The Gundersens were the first, or one of the first, city families to move to Big Hollow. Many more would come in succeeding years. The automobile, better roads and cheap land would hasten the exodus from the city to the nearby Catskills. At the end of the century, nearly all the descendants of the early settlers in Big Hollow would be gone. The farms would be abandoned, and fields and pastures returned to their natural state. The old homes and new ones would become occupied with city people, and a new way of life would prevail.

EBBY NEWCOMB

Down the old dirt valley road a short distance below the Phelps-Gundersen place was the old weather-beaten shack and barn of Ebby Newcomb. The buildings were back a little way from the road in a clearing surrounded by the woods. Ebby's wife, Pearl, had died and left him with three small children—Jay, Robert and Beulah.

Ebby was always ailing and complaining. He was not overly ambitious but he kept his little family together with no government assistance and with little help from his poor neighbors.

On the farm, there was a field of blueberries or huckleberries where great quantities grew. Each summer, the little family picked these berries and sold them to villagers for ten cents a quart. The money from these berries, together with his eggs, milk and pork, kept the family together and alive. Ebby sent the children to the one-room school about a mile down the road. Later, when the children were married and had homes of their own, Ebby moved down the valley to a little house near the bridge over the Batavia Kill and there he lived the rest of his days.

BEN DELONG

The third home down the valley was that of Ben DeLong. Ben was a big man with a big head, broad shoulders and a rather quiet manner. His home was on the left where the valley broadened out and where the stream was close to the road.

It is believed that when Ben was in his thirties, he advertised for a wife, which was a rather common thing to do at that time. Anyhow, a middle-aged woman from somewhere in the West appeared with her teenage son Arthur Smedley. Ben and Dessie were married and lived together for many years. Arthur attended the Windham High School.

Since the Batavia Kill creek in front of Ben's home abounded with big speckled brook trout, it was only natural that Ben became a skilled fisherman and brook trout was on his daily menu.

Big Hollow was and always had been a law-abiding neighborhood with little evidence of law or civil authority. In the 1920's, however, there was a game warden by the name of Art Riley who patrolled a large area of the Hunter and Windham Valleys riding horseback, later driving a model-T Ford car. Art was a dignified, austere officer of the law who was always in uniform and took his work of law enforcement very seriously. No one could understand how Art could patrol such a large area and appear so often and so unexpectedly in such unlikely places.

And then on a certain day, it happened. Art stepped out of the brush along the Batavia Kill where Ben was fishing. Alas, several of his trout fell short of the legal six inches in length. We saw Art and Ben go by in the open Ford. Someone said, "There, Art's caught Ben fishing." The Justice of the Peace in Hensonville fined him ten dollars, which would be equivalent to about a thousand dollars now. Poor man, all of his neighbors felt so sorry for him and would almost have enjoyed seeing a little misfortune overtake Art Riley, the game warden.

Since Art was about the only evidence of law enforcement in the Hollow, his presence in his khaki uniform and with his horse or open model-T Ford car with its top down caused concern.

Manley Mallory, for instance, had committed some minor misdemeanor which no one can remember. He was caught by Art, and as there was no Justice of the Peace in the Hollow, Manley had to appear before the Judge in Hensonville, three miles down the Batavia Kill Valley. Art started out riding his horse with Manley walking along beside him, when Manley suddenly exclaimed, "I'm not going to walk to Hensonville to be arrested!" Art pondered the matter for some time and became convinced the law favored Manley. So, he dismounted; ordered Manley to get on the horse and with Art leading the animal they made their way to Hensonville and back. Neighbors snickered and smiled at the pair: the officer in his slick uniform leading the horse on which was riding the culprit, Manley Mallory, in his shabby attire.

This amusing incident has been handed down from generation to generation showing in a simple but meaningful way that the individual citizen has rights which the law must respect.

THE MARTHA WEST FAMILY

At the turn of the century, there was no hospital in Catskill and the ones at Kingston and Albany were a long journey away. Local doctors were swamped day and night with house calls. They were good doctors and kind, sympathetic friends, but there was a limit to their endurance and knowledge.

One frequent cause of death at that time began as a pain in the stomach or on the right side. The doctor was not sure what caused it. The patient usually would continue to get worse and die. Later, it was learned that death was probably due to a ruptured appendix, which caused peritonitis and resulted in poisoning.

The farm below the Ben DeLong property was that of Martha West. The young husband, Adelbert, died of what was later diagnosed as a ruptured appendix. He left a young wife, Martha Ruland West, and six children: Charles, Nicholas, Lester, Leon, Laura and Lena. Leon was deaf and dumb. Martha was challenged with the big job of feeding the family from the run-down farm and keeping the children together.

Martha, who was the sister of George Ruland, was a strong-minded, wise lady with a lot of determination and ambition. And she soon had all the children working. There was wood to be cut, split and carried into the house; hens to feed and care for; cows to feed and milk; a garden to be planted and tended during the summer months; and hay to cut and draw to the barn for the cows and horses to eat during the winter months. The two girls were kept busy doing the housework, preparing meals, washing dishes, cleaning and canning fruit and vegetables. During the school year, the children walked with their lunch pails nearly a mile down the road to the one-room school. Leon went to a state school for the deaf at Batavia, New York.

Martha drove her horse and buckboard wagon to the local store and post office for groceries and her mail once or twice a month. She handled her spirited horse with a tight rein and in much the same manner in which she managed her children. On one occasion, as she approached the Hitchcock brothers' barn near the road where Jabez Barnum was threshing oats with a gasoline engine, the noise frightened the high-spirited horse which shied to one side of the road, knocking down pedestrian Charlotte Hitchcock and cutting her scalp across the forehead from ear to ear as the iron-tired wheel crashed over her head. She was carried to the Hitchcock home. Dr. Sidney Ford from Hensonville was immediately called and upon his arrival took many stitches to close the wound. Charlotte was in a coma for some time and not expected to live. She did finally recover, however, and lived for many years.

The Wests' childhood years slipped by quickly and pleasantly. As teenagers, they found some part-time work with neighboring farmers and thus helped with the family's expenses. Then came the time when they began to leave the old family home. Charles, the eldest, became a good carpenter, built a home for himself in Catskill and lived there with his wife. Lester became a truck driver and drove tractor-trailers for years. Laura married and moved away from the Hollow. Lena became a registered nurse. Nick and Leon remained at home with their mother, with Leon helping with the farm work and doing chores for neighbors. Eventually, he secured employment with the County Highway Department, married and moved to his own home in the Valley.

Nick secured the contract to haul milk from the farms in the Windham Valley to the milk creamery at Prattsville. He bought a big Graham Brothers platform truck with a Dodge Brothers motor and began the daily long haul of picking up 40-gallon milk cans at some 40 farms down the Valley and delivering them to the Prattsville Creamery. It proved to be a profitable business. Soon the old West house and barn were enlarged, modernized and painted. A large, two-car garage was built. The old place took on the appearance of a modern, up-to-date prosperous farm. Nick married and had three daughters. Martha, after a good and long life, passed away and was buried in the local cemetery. Nick continued to operate the farm for a few years, but died at a rather young age. His widow, Ella Davis, sold the farm to city people, who spend a part of their summers vacationing there.

THE MACGLASHANS

According to tradition, the MacGlashans emigrated from Scotland. A John MacGlashan is mentioned as a charter member of the Big Hollow Free Methodist Church in 1871. He even gave land for the church and helped to build it.

Down the valley a little way below the West farm and across the creek from the George Ruland farm was the MacGlashan homestead. William was a builder who could construct the frame for a barn with crude tools on the ground and, on a given day at a barn raising with local neighbors, erect the frame and roof which would fit together perfectly. William and Elizabeth had six children: Roy, Lyman, John, Orland, Nellie Rappelyea and Susan Butler. William and his sons and grandsons were skilled carpenters and mechanics.

Lyman, one of the older children, became a rather dramatic entertaining man. Returning from a visit to his brother Orland's in Nebraska, he narrated how the western trains traveled so fast that the telephone poles along the tracks appeared to look like a fine tooth comb. He also recounted how he had at times to fall on the floor of the train and cling to the carpet and furniture moorings as the train traveled so fast.

Lyman and his wife Lill West, who had no children, took loving care of Lyman's brother John, who was handicapped from birth, but lived to middle-aged manhood. Lyman was an interesting storyteller and people enjoyed listening to him. He smoked a crooked-stem pipe and in later years had what was then known as the ''shaking palsy.'' As Lyman sat in a well-cushioned old rocking chair telling a fanciful story or a personal experience, the attention of the listener would suddenly become diverted as Lyman decided to light his pipe. Holding it in his mouth with his shaking left hand, he would bring a lighted match in his quivering right hand to his pipe. With both hands, the pipe and match all in a shaking motion, it seemed a miracle that the pipe was lit. But it was and Lyman settled back in his chair comfortably relaxed to enjoy a few puffs and continue the narrative.

When Lyman's brother Roy, with his family, returned to the MacGlashan homestead, Lyman and Lill moved to the little house near the school house later occupied by George Irish and his family. Lyman and Lill's last years were relaxing and comfortable. Both lived to a good old age with many pleasant memories.

Roy MacGlashan was a versatile man, with many innate gifts. He was a builder, carpenter, and an excellent mechanic. While still a young man, he secured work on the Catskill-Cairo Railroad as the engineer. Later, he married and with his wife Evelyn returned to Big Hollow where he operated the MacGlashan Homestead farm and brought up their three children: Arlie, Edward and Milton. Roy and Evelyn also cared for John during the last years of his life. Arlie became a teacher. Edward, who was mechanical and operated sawmills with his father, later married Evelyn Crandell and moved to Chestertown in the Adirondacks where for many years he did a thriving lumbering business. Milton and his wife Antoinette Switter operated the home farm for years. They also developed a large maple syrup business and cut and sold wood fuel for a long time. Milton was a skilled carpenter and helped construct many buildings in the area.

Upon Roy's return from Catskill to Big Hollow and the MacGlashan homestead, he was soon in demand as a mechanic and carpenter. It was about this time that the State Board of Health required farmers to have concrete floors in their cow stables. And it was Roy MacGlashan who was hired by farmers in the area to do this difficult, dirty work. My father had a very old, 30-cow stable which has been used for probably 100 years. Roy knew just how to tear up the old boards, make the forms and do the foundation for the new concrete floor. He was also kept busy with his own machines and equipment, operating his saw mill, cutting wood, making maple syrup, and working as a mechanic for the highway departments of the Towns of Jewett and Windham.

When the Maplecrest-Hensonville road was hard-surfaced, Roy operated the steam roller. Jay Newcomb ran Roy's upright steam engine which provided power for the stone crusher located where Harry Hoyt's house now stands. And I drove Roy's team of horses drawing fieldstone to the crusher and crushed stone away from it to the road bed. Roy's son Milton estimates that his father possibly received $20 a day for these three services. The Otis Elevated Railroad at Haines Falls was in use summers from 1888 to 1919 and Roy was the chief engineer on this unique and famous inclined railroad as well.

When I was a small boy, I had built a concrete arch for boiling maple sap, but had no doors for it. I contacted Roy, a very busy man, to help me make doors for the arch. One morning he appeared early, looked at the arch, and mentioned that he had doors at home which would fit it. We drove up to his farm, got the iron doors and they fitted perfectly. But, to this day, I remember an important, busy man who helped a kid with a special project.

In the mid 1920's, the George MacGlashan family moved from South Jewett to another MacGlashan homestead about half a mile below the older one. They were distantly related to William's descendants. George and his wife Lola operated a farm in South Jewett where their three children, Ellen, Dorothy and Leon, were born. George had a brother Ory who operated the home farm for many years and then moved to a western state. There also were two sisters, Grace MacGlashan Peck and Margaret MacGlashan Hitchcock.

George and Lola managed their farm for many years with its good maple sugar bush and large house. During the summer months, they took city guests for board and room and in the autumn accommodated hunters who came to the valley deer-hunting. Ellen and Dorothy both worked in Albany in secretarial positions. They later married and retired to homes in Florida. Leon and wife Lillian Crandell have operated the farm, the maple business and the boarding house for many years following his parents' retirement and death.

GEORGE AND HATTIE RULAND

Across a short, low bridge over the Batavia Kill from the Roy MacGlashan farm and close to the main road, was the house and farm of George and Hattie Ruland. The wagon house was at the rear of the farm house, but the dairy barn was on a hill behind the other buildings. East of the house was a spring of cold mountain water which never ran dry.

George was the brother of Martha West and Hattie, the sister of John Irish, the cobbler. The Rulands had no children. George operated the farm which provided their livelihood. Hattie, a large woman, did the housework. Once or twice a month they would drive their team and two-seater surrey to the village with a few eggs or some butter to trade for groceries or cash. The horses, pulling with heads down, always seemed bent on running away, and George, sitting in the middle of the front seat with his feet braced against the dashboard, appeared to be always tugging and see-sawing with the reins to control them. Hattie, occupying the entire back seat, and weighing probably between 250 and 300 pounds, sat serene, like a queen enjoying the ride under the canopied top, totally unmindful of her husband's struggle with their wild, over-active horses.

At school tax time each fall, George became furious about paying his taxes, stating in angry terms that since he had no children he should not be required to pay any school tax. George had a mind of his own. He was stubborn, with strong, definite ideas, and could not be moved to change them. He also was rather suspicious of people and generally antagonistic toward the government, although as a neighbor and friend, he was always ready to give a helping hand. He was even an interesting conversationalist as long as the topics were light and casual.

In addition to the farm on the main road, the Rulands had a little, old, run-down farm with weather-beaten buildings on the Ruland-Hinman Road on the side of the mountain off the main road by the school house. In the winter when the supply of hay became exhausted on the home farm, George and Hattie would move with their live stock and a few necessary possessions up to the shack and old buildings on the mountainside farm where there was hay for the cows and horses. They would remain there until spring when the animals could find fresh grass for grazing.

George and Hattie lived a simple life. Both died at home and are buried in the Maplecrest Cemetery.

SAM AND MINERVA WEST

The Wests lived on the next farm down the valley from the Rulands. They, too, had no children. No one remembers about Sam's early life before coming to Maplecrest. It was reported that as a young man, he was quite musical and played the violin, guitar and fife in an orchestra on a riverboat plying the Hudson River between Albany and New York. For a number of years, he played the fife in a family orchestra with Jabez Barnum and his sons.

Sam was a little man—short and thin. When appearing in public, he wore a small felt hat with a narrow brim turned up. Sam drove a one-horse wagon to the village occasionally for groceries and mail. He usually had a bag of grain or some other object in the seat beside him. Sam believed this helped him avoid giving anyone a ride.

Minerva was a little woman with a noticeable limp. No one recalls ever seeing her out of the house or away from home. The Wests lived by themselves with almost no social life, as they had no telephone and no one was ever invited to their home.

When I was a boy, I once rode my bicycle up through the valley selling Cloverine salve for twenty-five cents a can. I called at the West home for a sale. After knocking at the kitchen door, I paused for some time and a little old wizened lady slowly opened the door, smiled, and asked what I wanted. I told her about the

Cloverine salve and its many uses. She silently withdrew into the room, returned with a quarter, took the salve, smiled and softly closed the door. I had never seen her before or since that time.

Leon MacGlashan, the Wests' next door neighbor, recalls how Sam talked to his horses as though they were people. Standing in front of a horse that wouldn't stand still, he'd shout, "You see that fist? If you don't stand still you're going to get it right between your eyes." At another time when Sam was cultivating corn, the horse stepped over the traces at the end of each corn row. Picking up a stick, Sam ran to the front of the horse, brandished the stick and hollered, "If you don't keep your darn feet within those traces, I'm going to knock your brains out with this club."

Sam and Minerva lived by themselves on their little farm for a long time. Sam had the butter money and Minerva, the egg money. When they passed away, each had saved two thousand dollars.

THE BETHUEL BARNUM FAMILY

On the Barnum-Ruland dirt road, which branched off to the left of the main valley road below the Goerge MacGlashan farm, was the school house of the upper Big Hollow school district. Beyond that was the farm of George and Hattie Ruland, and then a large farm where it is believed that Bethuel Clinton Barnum lived. He was the first Barnum in the Hollow; later, his son Jabez Barnum lived on this farm and then later still, Jabez's daughter Fannie with her husband Otis Planck and their family.

Little is known of Bethuel Clinton Barnum. He was born in Delaware County in 1820, moved to Lexington about 1845 and was a resident of Lexington in 1850 and 1855 as his name appeared on the census rolls for those years. It is believed that he lived in Prattsville about 1865, and that at a later date he moved to Big Hollow to the farm on the side of the mountain above what was later known as the George Ruland farm.

On May 2, 1844, Bethuel married Phoebe Julia Shoemaker and they had nine children; Phoebe died on August 13, 1864 at the age of 39. The next year, on February 19, 1865, Bethuel married Mary Magdalene Bunt and they had eight children. Of Bethuel's 17 children, seven of them settled in Big Hollow and four in neighboring East Jewett.

The Barnums were an affectionate, loving family. They enjoyed being together, visited one another often and, when separated, wrote to one another. Big Hollow became the center for the clan. Each autumn, in September, the Barnum Family Reunion became an important occasion when Barnums from far and near came together for a day, usually at the home of Jabez which was considered the family homestead. Allen and his family would come from Massachusetts; Frank's family from Kingston; and others from nearby places. The day would be spent visiting, eating, singing, playing games and attending a worship service. But most important of all was the opportunity to be together and renew family ties.

Jabez, who acquired the homestead down in the valley, was a most unusual and versatile man for his day. He was a good farmer with many acres of meadows, pasture and woodland. He enlarged the home and made it into a summer boardinghouse for entertaining city guests. At an early age, he had learned the stonemason trade and became skilled in erecting chimneys and building foundations and stone smokehouses for farmers to smoke their hams and bacon. Jabez augmented his income by making maple syrup and maple sugar to sell to local customers and dealers. He and his sons also cut stove wood to sell.

Jabez, the youngest and ninth child of Bethuel and Phoebe Barnum, was one of the first farmers in the Hollow to get an upright gasoline engine. It often took a lot of hand-cranking to get it started and then, for no reason at all, it would sometimes sputter and stop. Most of the time, however, it ran fairly well. The nearest place to get gasoline was at Horton Smith's in Hensonville. Horton had gas in barrels and would draw out five or 10 gallons as needed for the few engines in the neighborhood and for the even fewer automobiles. Jabez also purchased a threshing machine with which he would thresh oats and buckwheat for himself and farmers in the Hollow.

Jabez and his wife Elizabeth Bray Barnum had four strong, healthy sons and two pleasant hard-working daughters: Walter, Olin, William, Ralph, Fannie and Julia. Jabez and Lizzie taught their children to work at an early age and they all helped their parents with their many enterprises.

Since most city vacationers to the Catskills came on the Hudson River Dayline to Catskill, it was not surprising that Jabez soon had a seven-passenger Overland touring car for his son Ralph to drive to Catskill to meet city guests and to return them to the Dayline at Catskill at a later date.

Jabez was a natural musician. He could sing and play nearly every musical instrument. He taught his sons to play. The Barnum Family Band—made up of the four sons, Jabez and Sam West with his fife—often played at parties and picnics. There were drums, cymbals, a bass horn, trumpets and other horns which produced loud and spirited music.

The most conspicuous virtue of the Barnum family was their deep, religious faith. They were God-fearing people and for many years made up a large part of the congregation of the Methodist Church in Big Hollow. Jabez would go down through the Hollow on Sunday mornings with his four-seater wagon and family, picking up children and adults as he drove to church. His brothers Martin and Levi would be there, as would be his sisters Emma Crandell, Julia Rickard and Sarah Brainard. For many, many years, the members of the Barnum Family were officers in the church, Sunday school teachers and among the most faithful in attendance and support of the church.

Jabez was a born leader and promoter for his day in addition to being deeply religious. Whenever there was a death, an accident, sickness or tragedy of any kind in the Valley, Jabez was one of the first to appear, to offer advice and give personal loving help. Likewise, whenever there was a need for work of any kind, Jabez could do the job and usually better than anyone else. Also, at times of rejoicing—a birth, marriage, an anniversary or party—no one would be happier and enjoy the occasion more than Jabez.

The winter of 1922-23 was unusually severe with sub-zero weather and blizzards. It was my first year in high school at Windham. I drove our team of horses and sleigh the eight miles to Windham each morning for 62 days and was never once late at school. The few other students from Big Hollow and several from Hensonville would ride with me for $1.25 a week. At noon, Buell Morse from Jewett and I would go up to Coe's Hotel near the school to feed our horses at the hotel's stables. There was scarcely any car or truck travel during January and February. Only a few homes had radios.

The morning of February 12, 1923 was fair and a little warmer. After breakfast, Jabez, with sons Walter, Olin and Will, took their sharp axes and cross-cut saws to fell some trees back of the house, across the creek over by the sand bank. It was a short walk and the four men chatted and hummed as they trudged along, one behind the other in the bright, morning sunshine.

The first tree to be cut was notched so it would fall where desired for trimming off branches; the tree was surrounded by several small saplings. Walter and Olin began sawing opposite and slightly above the notch. Jabez and Will started cutting brush around the tree with their axes. Suddenly Walter shouted, "The tree's falling." It hit a sapling, whirled and fell on Jabez. The great weight of the tree came down on his head, crushing his skull. He died in Olin's arms.

As Buell and I were walking up Main Street in Windham at noon, someone shouted across the street from the hardware store that Jabez Barnum had been killed. A heavy weight fell on me. The sky seemed to darken. Uncle Jabez was dead. That night we saw Olin driving their team of horses by our house with Julia sitting on the floor of the sleigh. She had been away and was called back home. Jabez's death was so sudden and unexpected, it was unbelievable. The bereaved family, relatives, neighbors and friends were shocked and overcome with grief. Jabez Barnum, a great and good man, was gone at the age of 60. About a week after his death, Lizzie had a dream. She saw Jabez standing in the doorway saying, "Don't mourn. I am happy."

STERLING PLANCK

Although Jabez and Elizabeth had six children, they had only ten grandchildren. Among these was one destined to become unusually successful as a businessman.

Sterling, the oldest child of Otis and Fannie Barnum Planck, was born May 12, 1913 in Big Hollow. He was brought up by his grandparents, Jabez and Lizzie, graduated from Windham High School and Delhi State Agricultural College. This grandson was ambitious, adventuresome and possessed a fighting nature—to get an education, to get ahead and work for the common good.

During World War II he borrowed money to purchase buses, and transported workers to defense plants at Oneonta and Sydney. In 1946, he formed Planck Motors at Cortland. In 1957, he was awarded a trip to Hawaii for having the highest percentage of sales in the country. He was too busy to take the trip.

Sterling, in 1963, retired and moved to Florida. In 1966, he bought a boat factory in Hollywood, Florida; sold it within three years and purchased a large marina in Fort Lauderdale. Finally, in 1976, he sold the marina, vowing to really retire...but he still keeps busy.

He had three children, Sterling, Jr., and Dennis, who are businessmen in Cortland, New York, and a daughter, Phyllis, who lives in Florida.

Sterling has a home in Bonita Springs, Florida and another in Little York Lake, near Cortland. Here on the lake, he enjoys circling the shore line and waving to his many friends from his beautiful boat, aptly named, ''The Love Boat.''

THE MARTIN BARNUM FAMILY

Martin Monroe Barnum was the fourth child of Bethuel and Phoebe, and was born on July 12, 1845. He grew up to be a big man with a big head, big shoulders and a loud voice, yet with a sense of humor. Martin married Carrie Foster from Hensonville. Carrie was a small gentle woman with a loving spirit. She loved all people, flowers, birds and animals.

Martin and Carrie started life on an old, run-down farm with weather-beaten buildings on the Barnum Road, a branch of the Maplecrest Mountain Road. This road ran along the side of the mountains from the Maplecrest Road to Distin Hollow and on up to the eastern end of the Jewett Valley.

There were three old farms on the Maplecrest side of the mountain—the Abe Williams place, the Reuben DeLong homestead and the last and third was the home of Martin and Carrie.

Martin and Carrie were to have a troubled, sad life. Their first son, Albert, was born blind. He grew up to be a big man—a constant care to his loving mother. Albert had a good mind and could remember people by their voices and the smell of their clothing. He had the habit of always sitting down when the clock struck. Albert died at the age of 27.

The second child, Raymond, was born two years after Albert on March 4, 1893. Raymond was born an epileptic with frequent and severe seizures. He became a tall, handsome, well-built man with blond, curly hair. He married a Scottish woman named Mary Foster. He was a good carpenter and had local work for many years. He and his wife retired to Beacon, NY, where he died in 1966.

The McGlashan House

IS SITUATED on a large Farm high up in the CATSKILL MOUNTAINS, at an elevation of nearly 3,000 feet, and only a short distance from High Peak, Black Head, and Mt. Dome. Its high elevation and cool, bracing air render it a most healthy location for parties wishing a few weeks of perfect rest and quiet from the bustle of town life.

Good Accommodations for 25 Guests.

GENEROUS TABLE well supplied with fresh Milk, Butter, Eggs, and Vegetables from own Dairy and Farm. House strictly first-class. Comforts of home. No malaria. Daily mail.

Terms $6 to $7 Per Week.   No Hebrews Taken.

Special Rates to families and large parties.

Delightful Drives

AND MOUNTAIN CLIMBS especial attractions. Among them are Mt. Pisgah, High Peak, Devasego Falls, Haines Falls, Hotel Kaaterskill, Catskill Mountain House, Kaaterskill Falls, Black Dome, etc., etc.

Conveyances and careful drivers furnished by the Proprietor at reasonable rates.

How to Reach Us:

FROM NEW YORK TO KINGSTON by Kingston Night Boats, New York and Albany Day Boats, or by N. Y. C. RR. or West Shore RR.; from Kingston by the U. & D. RR., via Phœnicia, to Hunter. At Hunter, parties will be met with private conveyance, by notifying the Proprietor in advance. (By this route, from Phœnicia to Hunter, the traveler passes through the Stony Clove, a narrow pass where the mountains rise on either hand almost perpendicularly for nearly 2,000 feet.)

Any information desired cheerfully answered by addressing:

G. N. McGLASHAN, Prop'r, Big Hollow, Greene Co., N. Y.

Big Hollow basin (Maplecrest Valley), with Windham High Peak in background.

Big Hollow store around 1915 (site of today's post office). Road to East Jewett on left, road to Hensonville on right, Main Street and road through valley (Route 56) in front. Creamery in background far right.

Main Street, Route 56. Photo courtesy of Sugar Maples.

Maplecrest garage in 1950. Calvin DeLong with oxen. Will Vining in background.

Big Hollow blacksmith shop in 1932, with Elwood Morrow and blacksmith Mose Hitchcock.

The Maplecrest baseball team at a game with The House of David team on Sugar Maples ball field. Second Row: Elwood Hitchcock, Gerald Mackey (coach), Gerald Moseman, unknown, unknown, William Smith, unknown, Ray Osborn, Sheldon Peck, unknown, unknown, Frank Haner, Paul Mattoon, unknown, Walter Baker (umpire).

Crushing stone for the Maplecrest-Hensonville Road (Route 40), circa 1922, on the site of Harry Hoyt's house.

Ashley Hoyt, Ed and Cy Hoyt's father, at Barnum's homestead.

Platt Hitchcock's house and barns, 1886; currently the Wilfred C. Hitchcock home, Route 56.

Jerome Crandell's sawmill. Left to right: Walter Barnum, Ebbie Newcomb, Frank Hanley, Jerome Crandell, Manley Mallory, Calvin DeLong, Howard Crandell.

Big Hollow Men's Bible Club, Presbyterian church circa 1912. Front Row: Romaine Law, William Hitchcock, Mr. Distin (teacher), S.A. (Gus) Moseman, Raymond Moseman. Middle Row: Harold Hitchcock, William Vining, William Henry Moseman, Calvin DeLong, Dwight Hitchcock, John Planck, Merritt DeLong, unknown, unknown. Back Row: Jerome Crandell, Ed Winchell, Roswell Vining, Ed DeLong, Charles Phelps, Walter Bray, Vernon DeLong.

George Drum's barns enclosing a barnyard. George Drum and Jacob Planck holding horses. (Site of today's C. D. Lane Park, Route 56.)

First Free Methodist Church around 1900, Route 56 in village. Today a private residence.

A successful "coon" hunt, circa 1918. Alan Moss, Ray Osborn, Howard Crandell and dogs in front of the Crandell home on Peck Road.

Calvin DeLong on an oxen-pulled surrey.

Upper Big Hollow School in 1928, with all eleven pupils. Front Row: Deliah Schweir and Howard Crandell. 2nd Row: Lawrence Peck, Robert Rhodes, Doris Irish. 3rd Row: Kenneth Rhodes, Lillian Crandell, Mabel Schweir. Back Row: Emma Planck, Evelyn Crandell, Freda Schweir. Teacher, Ellen MacGlashan, in doorway.

Lower Big Hollow School in 1898. Rose Hitchcock, teacher. Photo includes: Grace Hitchcock, Gus Moseman, Pearl Moseman, Raymond Moseman, Harold Hitchcock, John Planck, Maurice Planck and Annie Garvey Hoyt.

Lower Big Hollow School around 1917, taught by Raymond Moseman. Front Row: Bernard Law, Cyrus Hoyt, Edwin Garvey, Winfred Rickard, Harry Hoyt, Edwin Hoyt. Middle Row: Eva Hitchcock, Vernette Moseman, Roger Rickard, Gerald Moseman, Birdsall Moseman, Leon Lewis. Back Row: Clementina Rickard, Katie Hoyt, Fredonia Moseman, Alda Bray, Viola Vining, Bertha Moseman, Nellie Law, Elwood Hitchcock, Lemuel Vining, Alfred Vining, Gerald Newcomb, William Hoyt.

Main Street with Sugar Maples dining room. Photo courtesy of Sugar Maples.

Snack bar and souvenir stand, Sugar Maples Resort. Fredonia Moseman at far left, Ray Lewis at far right. Photo courtesy of Sugar Maples.

Guests pose during "reverse party" at Sugar Maples Resort, July 1, 1942. Publisher's father, Merton Allen, is the tall svelte number in the tasteful striped ensemble in the back row, fifth from right.

Chief Crazy Bull (grandson of Chief Sitting Bull) with Sheila Meehan Getman and Thomas Patrick Meehan (today's Town of Windham Supervisor at Sugar Maples. Photo courtesy of the Meehan family.

Flora Barnum, Carrie and Martin's little daughter, was a beautiful child with the tender, loving qualities of her mother. She was admired and loved by everyone. The Barnum children walked over a mile down the mountain to the little schoolhouse below the Big Hollow post office. One rainy morning, the Barnum children arrived at the school early. The teacher refused to allow them to enter the building until the regular time. Flora, according to the story, caught cold which developed into pneumonia. She died at the age of 12.

Elmer, the youngest child in the family, was born July 2, 1898. Early in life, he developed a phobia about talking. This fear of talking remained with him until just a few years before his death in 1978. He would speak at home with his family and at school. He would talk until he reached the bridge by the post office; but he would never speak in the presence of strangers or anyone outside his family. Elmer conveyed his thoughts and feelings by nodding or shaking his head, smiling and laughing, or with a written note. No one ever heard Elmer talk until he was in his 70's, except two girls who hid behind the door at his home when he didn't know they were there as he began conversing with his mother.

Elmer was a great letter-writer, writing long letters on his philosophy of life and world conditions. Often he would write a special letter to be read at the annual Barnum family reunion.

Elmer liked people and enjoyed being with them. He enjoyed picnics and parties where he would laugh loudly and clap his hands with delight. He had a bachelor uncle, Levi, with whom he formed a close friendship. He also spent many evenings with his cousins, Robert and Linus Barnum, playing dominoes and eating great dishes of ice cream. Elmer was a big, strong man and hard worker. Summers, he rode his big Harley-Davidson motorcycle to work at the homes of city people in Onteora Park. After selling the Barnum farm, he moved into his cousins' home and lived there with them for several years before going into nursing homes. He died at the age of 79 and is buried in the Maplecrest Cemetery near his cousins Robert and Linus.

The strong faith of Martin and Carrie in God enabled them to live a contented and peaceful life. Martin died in 1927 at the age of 76 and Carrie in 1930 at the age of 72.

THE ALLEN BARNUM FAMILY

Allen was the eighth child of Bethuel and Phoebe. Unlike the other children, he was a little man—short and thin—but with a humorous spirit and a bright smile.

As I recall, Allen went to Massachusetts as a young man, driving a herd of cattle. He liked Massachusetts, got a job, married and lived there the rest of his life. Each year, he and his large family would attend the family reunion in Big Hollow. Almost before the car stopped, Allen's brothers and sisters would rush to the car and he would bound out. How they all would hug and kiss each other with tears flowing down their cheeks!

⤙ On October 20, 1968, Allen married Fannie E. Leffingwell, and, following in the steps of his parents, they had a large family. Seven children were born to them. Of these, Llewellyn and Harold occasionally visited their relatives in the Big Hollow area and they also entertained in their homes relatives from their father's home town.

Allen's second wife was Iona Warren, and they also had seven children. Of these, Irving, Bethuel, Crafton, Ruth and Milton became well-acquainted with their relatives in New York State. Ruth served as president of the family reunion as did Milton, who also prepared a genealogical research paper on the Barnum family.

The love and respect of the members of the Barnum family for one another is well-demonstrated by Allen Barnum and his children.

THE PECKS

Another bridge over the Batavia Kill west of the Barnum farm led to the Peck, Crandell and Chatfield farms on the north side of the creek, around where it is believed Deacon Lemuel settled with his family in 1795.

Newell Peck and Grace MacGlashan, his wife, had four children: Robert, Bessie, Sheldon and Lawrence. The Pecks were good people and good neighbors. When they learned in World War I that Robert was seriously ill of influenza and likely to die in one of the southern states, Newell started out on the long journey in his old model-T Ford to visit his son.

Newell and my father owned some 500 acres of pasture and woodland on the side of Windham High Peak. Each spring, for many years, Sheldon and I would leave school for two days to go with our fathers down to the Hudson River towns to get young cattle and dry cows to pasture during the summer months. This was a most exciting and enjoyable experience for us boys. There would sometimes be as many as one hundred head of cattle to drive along Route 23 from as far away as Coxsackie up to East Windham and then, turning left onto the old Ridge Road to the pasture on top of Elm Ridge. Often an old cow that had been to the mountain pasture for several summers would be in a hurry to get to the green grass and cool air again. She would go to the head of the herd and the others would follow along without straying off the road.

It seemed, though, that there was always a yearling heifer or young bull who wanted to get free of the herd and scamper to a nice, soft, fresh, green lawn. This action usually brought out an irate housewife waving her broom or an exasperated old man with his threatening cane, who would try to frighten the trespassing animal back onto the highway as they berated the drivers with a tongue-lashing.

One year, on a warm, May day as the herd was moving along quietly, a young bull suddenly decided to cool off in Green's Lake between Coxsackie and Leeds. He waded out into deep water, then turned around and looked at us as much as to say, ''Come and get me if you can.'' Ring, our faithful, hard-working dog, who saved us all so much running and shouting, would not swim out to the bull. Meanwhile, the herd was getting out of control with some grazing along both sides of the highway, and others striding ahead to get to the summer pasture as fast as possible. Luckily, as we stood at the edge of the lake wondering what to do, the bull suddenly began wading toward the shore and rejoined the herd, and we moved on.

Going down to the river towns each spring was something Sheldon and I looked forward to. It was a three-day vacation from school. We stayed overnight at some farmer's home with our fathers, usually at Mr. Scutter's near Coxsackie, listening to the evening conversation and rising early to get the drove started—getting a few cattle at one farmer's, some more at another, until we had all we could drive.

As we slowly moved along toward the mountains, old Ring would do most of the work running from one side of the road to the other, back and forth, and if one of the herd wandered astray, he was after it in a hurry and a couple of sharp nips in the heels brought it back. My father and Newell would follow along in the topless model-T Ford pick-up singing old hymns or visiting about old times. Sheldon and I each would ride on a front fender, making lines in the dust with our whips or jumping off occasionally to help Ring with a headstrong bull who was tired and determined to leave the herd.

Once the cattle were in the mountain pasture, it was necessary during the summer months to visit them biweekly. The cattle needed lots of water during the hot days of July and August, so the springs and brooks had to be examined to make sure there was a good supply. Cattle need salt, too, so we would carry ten to twenty pounds along to throw on smooth rocks for them to lick up. Then, also, it was important that they should all be accounted for. (Once, a young bull was missing and was later found dead in the crevice of a split ledge of rock where he had fallen or been pushed and had died of thirst and starvation.)

By the middle of October, we would begin getting the cattle together to drive back to their winter homes. The nights had begun to get cold and the grass was brown and dry. The cattle seemed anxious to get back home. They would walk along briskly with little or no attempt to leave the highway. As each group neared its home, the cattle would almost run and turn in to the driveway by themselves!

For several years, we also pastured a flock of two hundred sheep for a Mr. Bronwell of Climax, near Coxsackie. It was easy and fun to drive sheep as they would follow the leader straight to the pasture and in the autumn follow him straight back home. But bears and dogs killed so many sheep that we stopped pasturing them.

The increasing popularity of the automobile and the great number of cars on the highways put an end to driving a herd of a hundred cattle for twenty or thirty miles on State Highway Route 23. Thus, the era of summer mountain pasturing was ended.

The mountain land decreased in value with no income from pasturing summer cattle. (The income for all that work never exceeded a mere $500 anyway.) The trees for lumber had been cut years ago and the demand for wood as a fuel was decreasing, as coal and oil were being used more and more by village residents. So mountain land was practically worthless and the taxes on it were about nil.

It so happened in the early 1930's that the Conservation Department of New York State was buying mountain land and abandoned land in the Adirondack and Catskill Mountains. Along the south side of Windham High Peak and extending westward along what was known as the Ridge were some 2,000 acres of contiguous mountain land owned by five farmers: George MacGlashan, Newell Peck, William Hitchcock, Edward Haney of Hensonville and Zalom Hitchcock.

Edward West, an officer and surveyor in the State Conservation Department at Fleischmanns, was contacted and the State purchased the entire tract at six dollars an acre. During the winter of 1933-34, Edward and his crew of six men surveyed the big tract. The men boarded at our home during the week and returned to their homes in the Phoenicia Valley weekends. In the spring, the farmers received their checks from the State. My father's check was for $1,800, a small fortune for a farmer in the 1930's. The State lost no time in setting out evergreen trees in cleared areas and today it is impossible to walk through the evergreen forests where cows once peacefully grazed and sunned themselves.

As for the Pecks, Robert recovered from the "flu" and returned home from W.W.I. He built the Maplecrest garage and a new home, and married Gladys Davis, a school teacher in District #6 of East Jewett. Bessie worked in summer boardinghouses, in the school cafeteria and cared for her parents as long as they lived. Sheldon became an outstanding teacher at the Windham-Ashland-Jewett Central School and was also actively engaged in many community activities. He was an excellent baseball player and for years played on both the high school and Maplecrest teams. During his high school years, he assisted Val Morrow as a Boy Scout leader.

After completing college and teaching in the Maplecrest one-room school for several years, Sheldon married Ethel Beers of Prattsville and they established their home in Ashland about five miles west of Windham. They both taught school at Windham.

Sheldon continued his interest in the Boy Scouts and also became an active member of the Ashland Community Church. As a social studies teacher, he did much research on local history and life in the rural areas of New York State. Sheldon was a leader in the school's P.T.A., the Alumni Association and later served as president of the Greene County Retired Teachers Association. For some time he was Ashland town historian and with Flora Tompkins prepared a booklet on Ashland's history. Sheldon taught his pupils not only by precept, but even more importantly by example. He will long be remembered by his students and by his many friends.

Lawrence (Larry or Pete) married Frieda Lane of Ashland and took over the Peck Farm after his parents retired. He later worked for the town highway department before retiring to his village home in Maplecrest.

THE HOWARD CRANDELL FAMILY

The middle farm on the north side of the creek near the Peck Farm was owned by Howard Crandell. Uncle Howard was my mother's brother. He had married Carrie Drum, a sister of Fannie, Frankie and Maurice Drum. They had five children: Lucy, Evelyn, Lillian, Marie and Howard Jr.

Uncle Howard had a nice little farm and kept around 15 milk cows. He was a good carpenter; enjoyed fishing; worked some for his brother Jerome in his sawmill; and had a good sap bush which yielded wonderful maple syrup and maple butter each spring. For several years, in fact, I took their superior maple products to New Paltz where I had built up a good business with the faculty members of the State Normal School, which I attended in 1931-33.

During the 1920's, New York State began requiring dairy farmers to use greater care in the production of milk. These requirements were difficult for the small farmer. His cow stable was usually in an old barn. The stable had an old, broken, plank floor and wooden stanchions. During the winter months, the manure was thrown out windows behind the cows, and by spring had become huge frozen heaps. The cows were released from their stanchions once or twice a day to go to a trough in the barnyard for water, or to walk to a neighboring brook or creek. Some farmers had no milk house at all, but kept their night's milk at one end of the stable or outside, where it would be picked up with the morning's milk by the milk truck driver.

Renovating the stable was a big and dirty job. The old floor which had been down for years was often two or three planks thick in places with pools of urine underneath. The stanchions had to be ripped apart and everything had to be carried outside and carted away to burn. Then loads of gravel had to be brought in as a sub-base for the concrete floor. Building the forms for the concrete floor was rather difficult because of the gutter, the manger for hay, ensilage and grain, and the metal stanchion and drinking cups.

Renovating the old milk house or building a new one was time consuming and expensive. It was necessary to have running water, a vat for cooling the milk, racks for milking utensils and ventilation. It was often months before some farmers could meet all these requirements.

State milk inspectors came several times a year, unannounced, to examine the cow stable and the milk house. If they were found unsatisfactory, the farmer was prevented from sending his milk to the creamery until the improvements were made.

As soon as the inspector made his first stop at a farm in the valley, the farmer would rush to his telephone and notify the other farmers that the inspector was around and to get things in shape.

It so happened, one day, that Uncle Howard had his stable and milk house ready for inspection, but had no running water in the milk house. The inspector failed to observe this and went on to the barn to inspect the cow stable. Returning to his car, the inspector mentioned to Uncle Howard that he would like to stop in the milk house for a glass of water. Thinking fast, Uncle Howard asked if he wouldn't prefer to come to the house for a nice cool glass of apple cider. The inspector gladly accepted the offer and the day was saved.

The State also required all dairy herds of cattle to be tuberculin-tested. This was a simple procedure. A veterinary injected a serum under the cow's tail. He returned three days later to examine the animal. If there was a lump where the serum was injected, the cow had tuberculosis. Of the forty-five head in our dairy, twenty-two reacted. The State appraised the value of the cattle, paid the farmer a fair price and the diseased animals were disposed of. The herd thereafter would be examined periodically.

Lucy, Uncle Howard's eldest daughter, married David Irish, son of the Maplecrest cobbler, John Irish. For some years, Lucy and David operated the George Ruland farm. Later, they moved to the village into the house of David's parents, John and Josephine Irish. There, David worked for Sugar Maples as a carpenter and caretaker during the winter months.

Evelyn married Edward MacGlashan, son of Roy and Evelyn, and for a number of years Edward worked with his father in construction work and in the sawing of lumber. Later Edward and Evelyn moved to Chestertown in the Adirondacks where he purchased timber land, operated a big sawmill and did a lucrative business for many years.

Lillian, the third daughter, married Leon MacGlashan, son of George and Lola, and together they operated the MacGlashan farm and boardinghouse until their retirement.

Marie married Worthington Speenburgh of East Jewett and they settled in Haines Falls.

Howard Jr., the only son, married Olive (Peg) Pangman of Jewett and for several years ran the Crandell farm. Upon the sale of the farm, they both worked for a long time at the State Hospital in Poughkeepsie. Shortly after their early retirement they were both tragically killed in a motorcycle accident in Washington State.

THE CHATFIELD FAMILY

The third farm on the road across the creek was that of the Chatfields. It joined the Ridge Road from East Windham, which continued down the hill, across the creek and on over to the southern side to join the main valley road. At the junction of the roads was the Chatfield house and across from the house was probably the first one-room schoolhouse in the Hollow.

To this crude, rural school would come the three Irish boys—Lewis, David and George, who lived a mile up the Ridge Road; Robert and Bessie Peck; Lucy Crandell; Willis and Louise Chatfield and other children in the Valley.

Newcomb Chatfield was an only child of fairly well-to-do parents. It was said that he had attended a private military school as a boy. Be that as it may, he walked straight and tall with dignity. His speech was clear and articulate and he presented a professional appearance. Newcomb had one of the first two automobiles to come into the Hollow, probably around 1915. It was an open two-seater Stanley steamer. I remember Newcomb stopping one afternoon at our cows' watering trough for water. He put a long hose into the tub, turned several valves and the car began pumping water. When filled, it moved away almost silently, like a snowball rolling off a tin roof.

His wife, Grace Dunham from the Lexington area, was lively, dynamic and intelligent. They had two children, Willis and Louise. Raymond Moseman, a teacher of the old one-room school by the Chatfields, stated that the Chatfield children were among the most intelligent pupils he ever taught. Willis took over the farm when his parents retired to Hensonville. Louise married Leonard Vining and they had three sons—Leonard Jr., Gilbert and Burdette. Louise was burned to death while attempting to rescue one of her sons from their burning home.

Tradition has it that the Chatfield and Hitchcock ancestors once traded farms as the latter desired more fruit trees. Although there may not have been many fruit trees on the upper farm, there were certainly many blackberry patches in the pastures and woods. My father mentioned that as a young boy he had picked a pail full of the long, sweet juicy berries. Walking by the Chatfield home, Newcomb's mother inquired where he had picked them. He replied that he had found them in their pasture lot. She asked to take them. When she returned from the house, she handed my father an empty pail saying that since he had picked the berries on her land, they belonged to her. Although my father was a bit shocked and depressed, he had to agree.

Years later, Willis and his wife Dorcas (Cook) sold the farm to a Schwier family, who lived on the Old Road in Windham. The Schwiers made the old farm their home for many years. It was then sold to Kenneth and Larry Stewart, who developed a building project in the wooded tract north of the house. The C.D. Lane lake, a flood-water storage lake and recreational area, covers most of the flat land on the Chatfield farm.

THE GEORGE DRUM FAMILY

Across the valley from the Chatfield farm on the south side of the Batavia Kill was the large Drum farm. It extended all the way from the creek up across the valley road and on up into the mountain. June grass grew in most of the meadows as the land had lost much of its fertility.

The farm buildings a little distance below the junction of the Chatfield Road with the main road consisted of a large farmhouse and several farm buildings, joined together in the shape of the letter ''U.'' On the east was the wagon house in which were kept the farm wagons and road vehicles. At the rear was the hen house and attached to that, the pig pen. A long, low building at the rear of these three extended west and housed farm machinery, tools and other equipment. At the west end was a large building parallel to the three buildings on the east known as the cow barn with its hay lofts.

A stone wall along the highway enclosed the inside area of the farm buildings, making an ideal place for a barnyard for the cattle or horses to exercise. Doors on the buildings facing the enclosure made for easy accessibility and convenience for the farmer doing his morning and evening chores.

George Drum, as I remember him, was a short, rather stout, man with bleary eyes and a speech impediment. He had a sense of humor and enjoyed talking and telling stories and laughing uproariously. George and Lucy Clinton Drum had four children: Maurice, Carrie, Fannie and Frankie. Maurice married Emma Deyo of Westkill and they had two sons: Howard and Clinton. Carrie married Howard Crandell and lived on a farm between the Chatfields and Pecks. Their children were Lucy, Evelyn, Lillian, Marie and Howard, Jr. Fannie married Romaine Law and their children were Julia, Nellie, Bernard and Arthur. Romaine was the postmaster of Maplecrest for several years, operated the local grocery store and was organist in the Methodist Church. Later, he became a stonemason and was employed by Sugar Maples for many years. Frankie married Charles Garvey and they had two children, Edwin and Lydia. Edwin operated the Maplecrest garage for several years.

When I was teaching in the Maplecrest one-room school in 1933-1934, there were two little boys in the second grade around seven or eight years of age. Sterling Van was a cute, mischievous little boy and Clinton Drum, Maurice and Emma's younger son, was rather large and fat for his age. But the two young boys were great friends and were usually seen together.

During the noon hour, the older boys and I would often walk up to the Sugar Maples ball field in the village to play ball for a while. One nice day as we were on the bridge by the store, we saw my old model-T Ford pick-up truck slowly moving around the school grounds. The car continued to move until we had nearly reached the school. It then stopped abruptly and Clinton and Sterling took off on a run for the brush and woods up behind the school. My first thought was to take after them, but since it was nearly one o'clock I realized that if they were hiding I might not be able to find them, and I decided to start school. The boys stayed away all afternoon.

On the way home later that day, I met Sterling just below the Free Methodist Church plodding right along with his head down. I didn't stop and he didn't look up. A little farther up the road, I met Emma and Clinton. He was rubbing his eyes and trying to whimper. Emma, a large woman, was breathing hard and fanning herself as it was a warm day. The Drum farm was about a mile up the valley beyond where she lived. I stopped. After pausing to get her breath, Emma said, "The boy has done wrong and should be punished, Elwood, but I want you to know that when Clinton was born, he was a blue baby and the doctor thought he would not live for long." At hearing this from his mother, Clinton burst out into a mournful cry which ended in a dismal howl. I was sympathetic, but made no comment.

In a community where nothing very exciting ever happens more than a man getting stung by a bee or a horse running away, the school incident caused considerable excitement and speculation as to the outcome. The local telephones carried the news to every home in the valley.

The next morning after Bible reading, the Lord's prayer, Pledge of Allegiance and singing a few songs, I took my paddle and asked Sterling to come to the boys' room with me. The little fellow with lowered head and downcast eyes went ahead of me like a criminal on his last walk to the electric chair or the gas chamber. As we left the room, I saw Clinton give a wide, smug grin to the other children. I took Sterling across my knees, smoothed out his pants and gave him several light pats with the paddle. Then he stood up and I gave him a big hug and we returned to the classroom. After a pause for getting my breath, I quietly asked Clinton to come with me. A look of terror crossed his face as he looked from one side of the room to the other as if to say, "Something is wrong here! What's happened?" I gave Clinton a few sound whacks with the paddle as I believed he was more or less the leader in the incident, and also because he probably had never felt the sting of a paddle before. Clinton survived the punishment and lived to become a strong healthy man.

"Little George Drum" after his wife's death spent his last days with his daughter Carrie Crandell and family who lived near the Drum homestead. Son Maurice ran the farm for a few years, then sold it to Ray Osborn, who later sold it to Cyrus Hoyt and family. Today, three Hoyt families live in modern homes on the old Drum place, and a part of the farm has become the Clarence D. Lane Public Recreation Park and Lake.

THE PLANCKS

Across the road from the Zalmon Hitchcock home lived John and Ethel Planck, on a small farm which at one time had been a part of his father Jacob's farm. The house was small and close to the road and brook. The barn was old and had been used for storage, but John renovated it into a dairy barn for a few cows.

John and his older brother Maurice were the only children of Jacob and Ella Planck. The boys were not much like their father, as they were noticeably loud, bold and overly confident at times. They did not have a close relationship with their parents and would sometimes speak of them in a laughing, belittling manner. Also, the fact that Mr. and Mrs. Planck were seldom seen together in public except possibly at church or funerals gave the impression that they were somewhat incompatible, with strong, warring personalities, which caused their home life to be unhappy and miserable. This unpleasant family life existed, however, although Mr. and Mrs. Planck were devoted Christian people, good hard working neighbors, and good citizens.

Maurice, at a young age, married Ethel Vining of Hensonsville and moved to St. Remy, near Kingston, where he was employed as a superintendent on a wealthy man's estate. They had no children.

John married Ethel Sweet of Jewett and they had one child, a daughter named Emma. When she grew up, she married Russell Vermilyea of North Lexington. By this time, Mr. and Mrs. Jacob Planck had died and John and Ethel had taken over his father's farm, so Russell and Emma began operating the smaller farm of Emma's parents. As soon as John started running his father's farm, he and his hired man, Bert Beach, began slashing the hard maple trees in the maple sugar bush and selling the wood for fuel at a ridiculously low price. Although John improved the farm in some ways, the general condition of the land and buildings deteriorated.

After several years, John and Ethel left the farm and moved to the George Rickard property, which they had purchased. Russell and Emma and children, Glen, Joan and Eva, moved over to the big farm. They lived there for a while and then Ray Osborn bought it. He later sold it to Maurice Beers who, in turn, sold it to a city party.

Around 1955, Russell and his family migrated to Elsie, Michigan in the south central part of the state. He secured employment on the world's largest Holstein dairy farm. Emma died while they lived there and her body was brought to Windham for burial. Except for one or two visits, Russel and his children never returned East again.

The Planck family has now long been gone from the valley, but I shall never forget Mr. Planck. He was my close friend and made a lasting impression on my life.

THE ZALMON HITCHCOCK FAMILY

Down the valley a little way beyond the Drum place was the small farm of Zalmon Hitchcock, which he inherited from his father Austin Hitchcock. Zal was the grandson of Zalmon Hitchcock and the great grandson of Deacon Lemuel Hitchcock. Zal was an only son with three sisters—Charlotte, Florence and Mary. Florence, late in life, married William Hitchcock of Hensonville. Mary and Charlotte both married but had no children, and became widows at an early age. For her second husband, Mary married Gus Munson, a merchant in Ashland. Late in life, Zal married Rose Hitchcock, Platt's daughter and Will's sister, and had only one child, Austin.

The children of the Austin Hitchcock family line appeared to be a little more cultured and refined than the descendants of Platt's family. Zal was quiet and reserved. He was a medium-sized man who always stood tall and had a somewhat professional look. Zal was one of the few in Big Hollow who subscribed to the New York Tribune and kept informed about the news of the world. Rose taught school for more than 25 years.

Zal and his sisters were easy-going, likable, sociable people with a sense of humor. They were good visitors; good storytellers—people who enjoyed life, lived a day at a time and saw the good in people and the world. They didn't allow their daily work and mundane activities to interfere with the joy of living.

The two sisters, Mary and Charlotte, lived together for many years in the upstairs apartment of the Raymond Moseman house in the village. Once a week, on a nice afternoon, the sisters with shawls over their heads and shoulders and with a small milk pail would walk the mile up the Hollow to brother Zal's for their milk and a pleasant afternoon's visit with light refreshments with Rose and Zal in their sunny kitchen. The three sisters and their brother Zal were all much alike and enjoyed being together. They looked forward each Sunday to the services in the Presbyterian Church where they faithfully worshipped, and chatted with one another for a few minutes before and after the services.

Although Zal's farm was small, it was probably one of the best in the valley with a level, fertile meadow below the barn and another similar field across the creek. There was good pasturage for about a dozen cattle with a wood lot and blackberry patch and hard maples for producing maple syrup and maple sugar.

The farm buildings were old, unpainted and in the form of the letter "U" as were the Drum farm buildings. A little brook came down from the mountain, flowed under the highway bridge and along the west side of the house and barn and then on to the creek. When the Board of Health required farmers to have a milk house with running water, Uncle Zal built one over the brook. Unfortunately the brook often dried up during the summer months and as a necessary expedient, Uncle Zal brought his little herd of cows to our farm where each morning and night he came down to milk them and then put the milk in our vat of running water to keep it cool.

A nice lawn with beautiful maple trees was in front of their house which faced the road. As the house was built on a slight incline, the front was a little above the level of the road and the rear was several feet above the ground. The kitchen at the rear had a wood stove in the center and a window each side of it facing north; also a door leading out to the driveway and one on the west to the well-room. Here was the well curb for bringing up water in a large wooden pail, which was also used in the hot summer months for keeping milk, butter and other perishables cool just above the well water's surface.

Between the kitchen and the well-room were two paths—one leading to the little maple sugar house and the other to the hen house and the outdoor toilet. Inside, in front of the large, homey, warm kitchen was the big parlor with windows on the front and west. To the side of these two large rooms were two bedrooms, with several more upstairs.

At one time Zal's parents, Austin and Harriet Rowe Hitchcock, took in summer guests. It must have been a popular vacation spot as the food was delicious and plentiful; the house spotlessly clean; with outdoor farm activities and animals to watch; beautiful walks and a host family which was jovial, friendly and enjoyed chatting with folks in a leisurely manner.

It's said that an addicted drinker trying to break the habit was once watching Uncle Zal split wood, when he exclaimed, ''I would give my right arm if I could stop drinking.'' ''Put it on the block, and I'll rid you of it in a flash,'' replied Uncle Zal. The boarder gave a sickly smile, said nothing and continued to watch Uncle Zal split wood for the kitchen stove.

Austin, Zal and Rose's only child, was their pride and joy, also that of his three childless aunts, Charlotte, Mary and Florence. He was loved and given much attention; watched over; protected and bundled up well in winter. Austin became an unusually nice little boy, quiet, thoughtful, happy, agreeable and friendly. He learned easily in school and was sociable with the other children. At an early age it was observed that he was orderly, took good care of his possessions and did things well.

While just a young boy, Austin became a good trout fisherman in the Batavia Kill and learned to trap skunks in woodchuck holes when their pelts were bringing as much as six dollars each. With time and patience, he tried to teach me, his younger cousin by four years, where and how to fish and how to set traps so as to catch skunks. Unfortunately, I was a slow pupil and never managed the skills.

As Austin was mature and could be trusted, his father bought him a 32-calibre rifle when he was in his early teens. Aunt Rose, who had saved a little money from her teaching, bought him a beautiful new Ranger bicycle from one of the mail-order houses. My father and I brought it home from the railroad station in Hunter and assembled it on our front lawn. It seemed that all the children in the village and neighborhood were there to see the new bike. It was a beauty. Austin was down at our home and at his cousin Alice's often as he could ride back and forth quickly and easily. Occasionally, when he and Alice were playing croquet, I would grab the bike and go for a little spin. Austin had the bicycle for many years and it always looked like new—without a dent or scratch on it.

Somehow, Austin learned to play the pump organ quite well, and Aunt Rose bought him a beautiful, new mahogany organ which resembled a piano, although the latter was not yet in style.

Austin completed his requirements for high school graduation in three years and graduated from Windham High School in 1922 with two friends from Big Hollow—his cousins Scott Vining and Leonard Vining. That summer, he and Scott took a six-week teacher-training course at Oneonta State Normal School and in September Austin began teaching at the one-room school at Beaches Corners and, next year, at the two-teacher school in upper East Jewett. Scott taught both years in the upper Big Hollow one-room school district. It turned out, however, that neither cared for teaching. Austin's parents and aunts had great hopes and lofty dreams that with his character and talent he might aspire to become a university professor or some other notable person. But he seemed to like mechanical work and secured a job working in the Big Hollow garage for Robert Peck. Later, he and Scott took over a large gas station at the corner of Albany Avenue and Broadway in Kingston.

Meanwhile, Austin married Helen Campbell of Ashland, a former high school friend, and they made their home in Kingston. After a short time, Scott took over the gas station and Austin bought an old garage on the corner of Foxhall Avenue and Hasbrouck Street in Kingston. He was an excellent mechanic, absolutely honest and he built up a profitable business. They purchased a two-apartment house at 3 Delta Place, Kingston and lived there until Austin died in 1959 at the age of 55. They had no children. For many years, he and Helen had taken care of his mother, my Aunt Rose, until she died in 1948 at the age of 83.

Austin made many friends in Kingston in his business and in church. And he was always a good older cousin to me. His kindness and Christian example I shall never forget. He was the last descendant of the line of Zalmon, Deacon Lemuel's second son.

THE PLATT HITCHCOCK FAMILY

Coming on down the valley and down the hill from Mr. Planck's is the Hitchcock farm. Here the valley widens making a larger flat area for farm crops. At first the farm was small, but over the years it was enlarged to include two maple bushes; the abandoned Davis farm on the old East Windham road; and three hundred acres of woodland and pasture land on the south side of Windham High Peak adjoining a similar two hundred-acre tract owned by Newell Peck.

It was said that in the early days the Chatfield family owned the present Hitchcock farm and the Atwaters lived up near the Crandell and Peck farms on what later became known as the Chatfield farm. But, because of the many fruit trees on the lower farm which the Atwaters desired, they traded farms with the Chatfields and moved to the present Hitchcock farm site.

When Platt Hitchcock, 1832-1915, Deacon Lemuel's grandson, married Emerett Atwater in 1856, the farm was small and neglected. Not much is known of Emerett's parents. Apparently, Platt and Emerett took over the farm. Over the years from 1861 until 1879 they had six children. One, a daughter Ella, died a few months after birth; and another daughter, Eva, who obtained a college education in Albany, taught school for a few years, became engaged to a Frank Sillman of Hobart, but then became stricken and died at a young age just a few weeks before her wedding date.

The other four children lived to a ripe old age. Rose married Zalmon Hitchcock and had one son, Austin. Dwight married Margaret MacGlashan and had Alice and Herbert. Julia married Roswell Vining and had three sons: Scott, Robert and Alfred. William married Grace Crandell and had four children: Elwood, Edwin, Eva and Wilfred. All four families lived on their farms in the valley most of their lives and were faithful members of the Presbyterian Church.

Platt looked like an old man for most of his life. It was said that he had worked himself out as a young man. Although he was a hard worker, he wasn't much of a businessman or farmer. (When the children were small, he even had to buy milk from his neighbor Mr. Planck, for his family.) He was, however, a scholarly man, interested in reading and learning. He spent much time in Bible study. He was interested in phrenology. As a little boy, I remember he once took me between his knees and with his long fingertips studied the formation of my skull. Obviously, he must have been disappointed as he never repeated the examination.

He was once chosen to represent the Mountain Top Presbyterian churches at an important National Synod meeting in Chicago with all expenses paid. Upon his return, a meeting was called to hear his report, but he was so shy and timid he was unable to speak. Platt was a dedicated leader in the Presbyterian Church. I attended that church until 1938, when I was married and moved away to Saugerties to teach school. For 17 years I had served in the church as janitor at 25 cents a Sunday. In all those years from young childhood I can never recall a single Sunday that my parents were not at church for both the Sunday school and worship services along with the other Hitchcocks.

Emerett was a quiet little woman—a good wife and mother. At one time she had a mental disorder and was in an institution for a short time. She nevertheless lived to be an old lady and following her death there were found in a bureau drawer four rolls of $500, one for each of her four children.

The old farmhouse was small and poorly built for so large a family. Snow often blew into the upstairs bedrooms. In 1900, Platt's brother Dwight of Windham built for the family a large new house where the present one stands at a cost of $6,000. It had a stone cellar floor under the entire house, two stories, with a large open attic on the third floor. However, by this time, some of the children had married and moved away and so large a house wasn't needed.

Platt and Emerett moved into the new house, and when Dwight and Margaret were married they moved into the old house. Later, when Will and Grace were married in 1904, they moved into part of the new house with Platt and Emerett, and Grace helped to care for them as long as they lived.

Grace Crandell and William Hitchcock were married on the Will Reynolds Farm, Goshen Street, Jewett, on November 9, 1904. Grace and Will raised four children and worked hard together on the farm in Big Hollow for 62 years. Most of those years were happy and good, but some were hard and almost unbearable.

At the age of 18, Grace moved into the newest, largest and probably the most beautiful house in the Valley. She withdrew her membership from the Methodist Church of her mother and joined the Presbyterian Church of which her husband was a member. She became a Hitchcock and a good Presbyterian for the rest of her life.

Shortly after my parents' marriage, my mother saw a letter written by her sister-in-law in which she mentioned that Willie could have done much better in his marriage. This greatly upset mother, who was well aware she had married into a family several social steps above her own. Her father, Billy Crandell, and at least one brother enjoyed a glass of hard cider now and then. Both kept barrels of the stuff in the cellar. They also smoked and seldom, if ever, stepped inside a church!

The Hitchcock family, on the other hand, was the oldest and supposedly the best established family in Big Hollow. Was not Willie a member of the fourth generation of Hitchcocks? He was the son of Platt, who was the son of Jason, who was the son of Deacon Lemuel, the first settler to Big Hollow in 1795.

Mother became determined that she would prove she was a good wife and mother. This goal she worked toward all her life and succeeded well in spite of untold hardships and almost unbearable sorrow until she died in 1966 at the age of 79.

It would always be a busy household for Grace and Will with their four children: Elwood, born in 1908; Edwin, 1910; Eva, 1912; and Wilfred, 1919. Edwin was sickly with eczema and asthma from almost the time he was born, and Grace would spend many nights fanning him to help him breathe. He was never well enough to attend school regularly or to do much work.

Then, too, Mother's only daughter Eva, had married Donald Thompson of Windham on October 30, 1930. In the next few years, they had four sons: Herbert, William, Donald Jr. and Robert. Their home was on Main Street, Windham with Donald's mother, Mame, living in the adjoining apartment. On August 17, 1944, Eva, at age 32, suddenly and unexpectedly took her life, leaving her husband and the four little sons, ages 7 to 13. Shortly thereafter, Grace and Will moved into Eva's home to care for her family until a lady was employed to take over the household duties.

It was generally accepted that even though Will appeared healthy and strong, in reality he was thought to be of a frail nature and had to be waited on, had to have his necktie tied and his shoes shined for Sunday church services. And, of course, he couldn't be expected to help with household chores or even with disciplining the children as he had all he could or should do with the farm work.

Unfortunately, too, Aunt Rose was troubled with indigestion and could only do the minimum household work; and Aunt Julia had a large tumor which incapacitated her. So, the task of entertaining church visitors, relatives of the Hitchcock clan and others fell on poor Grace. She was also expected to teach a Sunday school class and play the organ in church.

In 1915, Will and his brother Dwight finally decided to take over the family farm by buying their sisters' share of it. They formed a partnership known as The Hitchcock Brothers. Will had worked on the farm for his father for no wages until he was 21. Dwight was a businessman interested in dealing in cattle, sheep and hogs. A slaughter house was built and he became a butcher and meat dealer, as well. Will liked farm work—caring for cattle and working the land. He was nicknamed ''Scrubby,'' and Dwight, ''Ezra.'' The business and farm grew and prospered. They were good years for the two young families.

The big dairy farm, with a herd of 30 milking cows, was between the two houses with the wagon house and four horses across the road from it. At noon, during the summer months, Aunt Maggie and Alice would come from their house with a pail of water and my mother and I from our house to the milk house to wash the milk cans and pails. Alice and I would often make mud pies and put them in the cracks of the stonewall to dry.

Then tragedy struck. Uncle Dwight had a small ''bunch'' come on his neck. He treated it with home-made remedies, then went to Binghamton and Albany for diagnosis and treatment. But the cancer continued to grow. For nearly three years, Uncle Dwight suffered. Then, in 1918, at the age of 43, he died, leaving a widow and two small children.

For a year or two, Aunt Maggie hired a man to take Uncle Dwight's place, but the plan didn't work well and in 1920, Pa bought her share of the farm with the livestock and farm machinery for $5,000. Aunt Maggie purchased a boarding house in Windham and later married James Cryne. Alice later married Claude Campbell of Ashland; and Herbert, Doris Woodworth of Hensonville.

In addition to the buildings and farm animals and equipment, the sale of the farm included 300 acres of woodland on the south side of Windham High Peak and another 100 acres of wood, pastures, meadow and cropland.

We owned the farm! It was all paid for, but there was no money left. It had taken every nickel of Pa's money. He was 42 on March 20, 1920, and I was 12 on March 22. We were both in our prime. We went to work. We were to work together side by side as father and son for the next 18 years. And those were among the happiest and most rewarding years of my life.

As my father was the youngest of five children and had been born when both his parents were over 40, he had been pampered by them and by his older sisters, who had given him the nickname of "Willie." Then, too, when he was a boy, he had had several attacks of epilepsy which caused his family and friends to believe he might have more seizures. Thus, his family and his wife were always concerned about his health and his becoming over-tired. My mother waited on him and protected him as though he were a child until she died.

My father's farm work was very important to him. He had a definite schedule and he tried always to be ahead of his work, to push his work and not let the work push him. He therefore had his fence stakes cut and sharpened long before it was time to repair the fences. The milk was always ready long before the truck came for it.

It seemed, too, that the work he planned for the morning would always be a little more than we could easily do, so we would hurry and work right up until noon or later and then in the afternoon it was much the same—work fast and hard until chore time.

Not so with my mother, who had a large house to take care of. Alvena and I often wondered if a carpenter or anyone had planned it or whether it just fell together: The kitchen had no cupboards. The sink was in the pantry, which also had no cupboards. Frying pans, dishes and food were stored in the cellar-way, down cellar or in the back room. So it was difficult for mother to do her work with so much running around, and her feet always hurt her. Then, too, she had four children to care for and her in-laws to help as well as work to do in the church.

I am reminded of Madge Van Slyke of Hensonville, who once remarked that she never saw her mother walk in their kitchen as she always went on a trot from stove to cupboard and sink to table. I never saw Mother run, but she often would not have meals ready at the established hours of 7:00, 12:00 and 5:00. When this happened, Pa would sit down and begin eating bread and milk and continue with the other food as it was brought to the table.

Pa was also a perfectionist with his farm work. The crop land was plowed in the fall with a side-hill plow. During the winter months, it was covered with cow manure and then in the spring it was harrowed several times with a horse-drawn, walking, spring-tooth harrow. When the land was ready for corn, the main crop, it was marked out with a horse-drawn, three-tooth marker. The marker was drawn along the edge of the field and then on the way back, one tooth would follow in the outside marked line and would make two new rows. This would be repeated until the entire field was marked out.

At last, the big field was ready to be planted. The old horse-drawn, one-row walking planter was brought out. It contained two bins—one for the seed corn with a generous covering of tar on it to dull the crows' appetite for it, and the other for fertilizer. As the corn and fertilizer fell into the row, a concave shoe brought in the dirt from each side of the row and covered the corn and fertilizer as a large wide flat wheel at the rear of the planter pressed the dirt down on the row.

After the corn had started coming up, there would be empty spaces in some of the rows with no corn, or there would be weeds and quack grass. To take care of this, more corn would be mixed with tar in a bucket, emptied into a paper bag, put in Pa's overalls pocket, and he would fill the empty spaces in the rows with his hoe, cover the corn and dig out the weeds.

When it came to cultivating between the rows, we had a horse-drawn, one-row walking cultivator. I would ride the horse, guiding him between the rows, while Pa guided the cultivator. On warm days when the horse sweated and the flies bothered him, my pants would get so wet with sweat and horse hair that I would get off and lead him until I got tired and then get back on. Some years, it would seem that there was so much quack grass and weeds that Pa felt we should go twice between each row—once close to the right row and on the return keeping close to the other row. This was boring, tiring work, but in September there would be enough corn to fill two silos!

As I look back, I realize Pa took good care of his health—always eating at meal time, seldom between meals and rarely sitting in a chair except for meals. We usually had an old sofa in the kitchen with a floor lamp by it. When the milking was done after supper, he would lie down and read magazines until bedtime at 9:00 o'clock. He left the care of the children to Mother, and she had her hands full.

Ed's asthma prevented him from being near farm animals or doing hard work. It was also believed that we couldn't afford to hire outside help except in the maple syrup season and for harvesting the hay during the summer. So, to get the work done, Pa would get up at 4:00 a.m. during the summer months and at 5:00 a.m. during the winter. I would get up a little later and we would get the chores done and horses harnessed for the day's work before I rushed off to school. In the afternoon, I would hurry home from school, quickly change my clothes and rush out to the barn to help Pa with the evening chores and finish up the day's work.

And so it went from year to year—working together, Saturdays and vacations, cutting wood in the mountains and in the summer filling the big barns with hay for the cows and horses. During many of those summers, we would do a day's work before noon, so we could play baseball in the afternoon.

We worked hard together and didn't talk much. When milking, we would hum and sing together the old hymns of the church. Pa loved to sing and would do so when working in the field, drawing wood, and even drawing grain from Hunter for the cows. Pa also was a great reader. By reading farm papers, he became a progressive farmer. He also enjoyed newspapers and magazines.

As there was little social life in Big Hollow, families kept much to themselves and became rather self-conscious in the presence of strangers. Pa was shy and timid in public, but at other times was confident and outgoing. I, too, was bashful and timid. I well remember in 1922, when I was 14, we had just bought our first model-T Ford touring car. We had driven to Catskill and parked on Main Street opposite the Catskill Savings Bank. It seemed that Pa always enjoyed visiting places where he had a few acquaintances. He was sure of himself and "felt his oats." He would buy a bag of popcorn or peanuts and walk down the street, chewing away and throwing peanut shucks everywhere.

On one particular day, he was sitting in the back seat of the Ford on the street side. He had never learned to drive. I was in front behind the wheel. It was a warm day and Pa settled down and began eating peanuts and throwing the shells out into the street. He was a little impatient waiting for Mother and the children. He began eating peanuts at a furious rate and throwing out the shells in almost a continuous stream.

I looked at the place in the street where the shucks were landing and to my horror saw a small pyramid of shucks growing higher and higher on the clean brick pavement. I broke out in a cold sweat as I thought of a policeman coming along and making Pa get out and clean up the mess on his hands and knees, or worse still being put in the County jail or paying a fine for littering.

Another time, I was embarrassed was in the spring of 1927 at Delhi. I had been accepted at the Delhi State Teacher Training Class and we had driven out to get a room for the coming September. After we had finished our lunch in a little diner in Delhi, Pa asked for the check, which, as I look back was not unreasonable. But, I think, perhaps the waiter was new and inexperienced, for he appeared a few minutes later with a check book on the Delhi bank. I was mortified and left the diner immediately wondering how the problem would be settled.

Pa smoked cigarettes for many years before we knew about it. For a long time, I smelled tobacco smoke in the barn and was always disturbed as I thought some tramp or stranger was going into the barn and might set it on fire. One day, I happened to see him going from one barn to the other with a bucket of sawdust. In his mouth was a little black, crooked stem pipe that children used to play with and in its bowl was a lighted cigarette sticking up just beyond his nose. And he was puffing away for all he was worth. Another time, I caught Pa smoking as he was feeding grain to the cows. Seeing me, he quickly plunged the cigarette into the grain.

Although Mother's father and brothers were great smokers, she gave Pa a hard time, sputtering how it would ruin his health and that he was a bad example for his three sons. After many years, he became comfortable smoking in the house and in the presence of his family. When his grandson, Billy, was in the Navy as a pilot on the Intrepid aircraft carrier, he would bring Pa several cartons of cigarettes at a time when he could purchase them for a dollar a carton. Pa greatly appreciated Billy's thoughtfulness.

When Pa was approaching 90, we would sometimes see him on a hot summer's day sitting in a rocking chair in the woodshed puffing away on one cigarette while holding another lighted one in his other hand.

The last years of Grace and Will's lives were easier. Their three sons had married happily and there were grandchildren. Son Wilfred worked on the farm for many years with his father and then when he and Iris Finch were married in 1940, moved into the big house with his parents. In the 1950's, Wilfred and Iris bought the farm and Will worked with Wilfred for many years doing light work, and he enjoyed watching the farm grow and prosper under their management.

Grace and Will enjoyed visiting. They visited their niece Lucy Irish and family for a few days; also Alice and Claude Campbell in Ashland; Evelyn and Ed MacGlashan in Chestertown; and son Elwood and family in Margaretville or Dolgeville.

In later years, Will believed he had heart trouble and had to be extremely careful not to exert himself. He required even more attention and medication. He would take as many as 17 aspirin tablets a day. He even went upstairs backwards as he believed that was easier on his heart. Grace was subject to his call 24 hours a day. One night in March 1966, he thought he was dying and asked Grace, who had become quite feeble by this time, to go to the foot of the stairs and call Wilfred to come down. She got out of the bed and into a rocking chair which she zig-zagged across the room and had nearly reached the foot of the stairs when she became desperately ill with a stroke. Several days later she went into a coma from which she never recovered. She died on March 26, 1966 at the age of 79.

Grace Crandell Hitchcock was a good wife and a good mother. She loved all of us and showed her love by the time and attention she gave us. I never heard her raise her voice or scold one of us. She was of a cheerful nature and laughed easily. She didn't complain or grumble about her lot in life, but accepted it as it came to her. She was a good example for us. We were fortunate to have her for a mother.

Pa, also, was a great influence on my life. He was gentle, kind, easy-going and flexible. He gave us children freedom and independence. I don't recall that he ever scolded us and usually went along with our requests and desires. He died quietly on the farm where he was born on April 27, 1972, at the age of 94. Pa was a good Christian man and a wonderful father.

THE FAMILIES ON THE SLATER ROAD

A little distance below the Hitchcock farm, the Slater Road branched off to the right across the Batavia Kill. For many years there were four families living on this hill road.

Henry Slater and his wife lived at the top of the hill. Henry was a big, fat, jovial fellow with several gold teeth. He never seemed to have much to do. Later in life, he and Sid Van did concrete construction work for several summers. Henry died in Florida. A city family by the name of Phillips purchased the Slater place and lived there several summers until the house burned.

To the left of the Slater Road, at the top of the hill, was the farm of Anson Hitchcock and his wife. They boarded guests during the summer months, made maple syrup from their little sap bush and kept a few cows, some hens and a pig or two for food. I drove our cows to day pasture by their house and often would chat with them.

Sometimes I would ride with Anson in his old buggy wagon pulled by his old skinny horse. Anson chewed tobacco and was a good storyteller. Once he inveigled me into disposing of five of his kittens for five cents.

The Anson Hitchcock farm house was on a high elevation on the hill and commanded a spacious and beautiful view of the Big Hollow valley. After Anson's death, Sarah Brainard had the house dismantled and rebuilt near the home of her brother, Jabez Barnum, two miles up the valley.

Beyond the Slater place on the hill was the home of Charlie and Jennie Newcomb and their five children: Violet, Jessie, Norma, Charlie and Gerald. Charlie was a little man and supported his family by cutting wood alone with an axe and buck saw and drawing it to Hensonville or Windham for three dollars a cord. Charlie was a brother of Ebby who lived three miles up the Hollow with his family. Jennie was a big, strong-minded woman who kept Charlie and the children busy.

The farm had once belonged to Dr. Sidney Ford's father and in the barn was a human skeleton which Sidney had studied while a student in Albany Medical College. With no welfare assistance and not much help from the poor neighbors, Charlie and Jennie managed to bring up their children, who turned out to become good American citizens.

The first house on the Slater Road was the home of Billy and Emma Crandell. It was a nice little side hill farm of a few acres with a cow barn, hen house, pig pen, shop and outdoor toilet. The house was small with low ceilings and little rooms, but it was a warm, comfortable house.

Billy was a short man who wore his hat all the time, indoors and out. He smoked Bluebird tobacco in his corn cob pipe most of the time. I never saw him read. He put two or three barrels of cider in the cellar each fall, but was a temperate drinker. He had no teeth. In addition to operating his little farm, he occasionally did carpenter work for the neighbors and with his earnings would then take life easy for a while.

Grandma Crandell was a large woman—industrious, intelligent and religious. She was the daughter of Bethuel Barnum. When she married Grandpa, he was a farm hand and told her that he had saved money for starting a home. She later learned this was untrue and that he had even borrowed a suit of clothes to wear to their wedding. They had three children: Jerome, Howard and Grace.

Grandma took in washings to enable Grace to take organ lessons. She took Grace to church and Sunday school with her every Sunday. She encouraged Grace to do her best in school and to become a refined lady.

In addition to her home life, Grandma was a dedicated member of the Big Hollow Methodist Church, teaching Sunday school classes most of her life and attending mid-week prayer meetings.

To help support her family, she made butter by skimming the cream from pans of milk and then churning it into butter in a hand-operated up-and-down churn. Her few pounds of butter were in great demand by regular customers in the village. Later, she began taking summer boarders. She was an excellent cook, immaculate housekeeper and a genial hostess. Soon she had more guests than she could accommodate and had to rent sleeping rooms in nearby neighbors' homes.

Her work was unbelievably hard. There was no indoor plumbing, no electric lights, no dishwasher or washing machine—just tubs and the scrub board. For Sunday dinner the rooster had to be killed, picked and cooked. The ice cream had to be made and frozen in the hand freezer. Meals were cooked on an old wood burning range and were served family-style. There were no chambermaids or waitresses. Grandma did all the work. The summer rates were ridiculously low—perhaps ten dollars a week or a dollar a day for a room and three big meals a day.

As I was the oldest grandson of Grandpa and Grandma Crandell, and since their home was only a short distance across the bridge from ours, I spent much time with them. Once when I was stuttering, I was sent to spend some time with them in the quiet, peaceful atmosphere of their home. Another time, Grandma caught me smoking one of Grandpa's pipes. She made me keep smoking 'till I was so dizzy the whole world seemed to reel about me and I felt I was vomiting up all I had ever eaten. I've never had the desire to smoke since then.

On another occasion, Grandma told me about the great P.T. Barnum, one of her ancestors, who formed the world-famous circus known by his name. He also trained President Woodrow Wilson to deliver his inaugural address.

In the twilight of the day after supper, Grandpa would sit in his armchair by the stove, smoking his pipe with little clouds of smoke drifting over the stove. Grandma would sit in her rocking chair. There was silence in the room except for the ticking of the old clock on the mantel. As darkness descended, Grandma would light the oil lamp on the table with a rolled paper from the fire in the stove. Stillness, peace and contentment would again reign until bedtime and the close of the day. But there was something in that twilight hour that was powerful and lingered on.

JOHN HAYNES

John Haynes' farm was at the eastern end of the village across from the old Free Methodist Church. It was a good farm with a large flat, big meadows, a good maple bush and a wood lot.

Mr. Haynes was a little man, a hard worker, rising at four and five in the morning to begin his daily work. He was very thrifty. His wife was Alice Planck, Mr. Jake Planck's sister, and she and John had no children.

At the front-west corner of the Haynes house was a shallow well—15 or 20 feet deep. It had been dug by hand labor and laid up with local stone. It was an important source of water to the Haynes family. The only other water available for the farm animals was a brook running through the pasture lot some distance east of the horse stable and dairy barn. When this brook occasionally dried up, Mr. Haynes had to carry all the water from the well, not only for the household but for the horses and cows as well.

A yoke over his shoulders with ropes and hooks at either end for the pail handles helped Mr. Haynes carry the heavy pails of water. During Mr. Haynes' long life, he never had the benefit of electricity, a water pump, or pipes bringing water to his buildings down from a mountain spring. Mr. Haynes never had a wood shed, but piled his wood in the back yard where it was kept dry and seasoned by old boards on the top of the piles. During the winter, he carried this wood across the yard and up the steps to the kitchen wood box.

As little farm labor as possible was hired except for harvesting hay and making maple syrup. Mr. Haynes would work during the day, cutting the hay, making and piling it, then he would hire someone like Calvin DeLong, who had another job, to come and help him draw the hay to the barn in the late afternoon and evening.

One summer afternoon when a little sprinkle had begun to fall, Mr. Haynes was seen running across the field to the house. Soon he was back with his old straw hat. He didn't want his new one, which had probably cost 25 cents, to get wet.

Although nearly every farmer in the valley had a Grimm evaporator with corrugated pans to boil maple sap, Mr. Haynes stuck to the old stone arch with flat bottom pans to boil the sap into syrup slowly.

One day following a good sap run with the buckets running over and the snow quite deep and still snowing, Mr. Haynes decided it wasn't a fit day to take the horses out in the storm. So my father-in-law, Merritt DeLong, his hired man, and Mr. Haynes waded through knee-deep snow in the storm all day long with pails carrying sap from each bucket to the sap house. The stabled horses stayed warm and dry. Mr. Haynes and Merritt were soaking wet and exhausted. That night at the supper table Merritt had enough energy left to murmur, ''Mr. Haynes, never again. If the weather isn't fit for the horses to be out, it's not fit for me either.''

Since Mr. Haynes purchased very little commercial grain for his horses and cows, the horses became thin and weak; the cows didn't produce much milk; and neither was there much manure for the fields and they became unproductive.

As the horses became older and their teeth wore down, Mr. Haynes cut up poor hay into short pieces and mixed it with a little grain and water for the horses' nourishment. In the cold winter, he placed a blanket on the horses under their harnesses to keep them well and warm.

The little cows became scrawny and wild because they seldom saw anybody but Mr. Haynes. As Mr. Haynes had no milk house or running water to keep his milk cool, he arranged with my father to put his milk in our cans with our milk. This project required a great deal of work for him. After he had milked the cows, he would strain the milk and measure it. Next he would carry the two dish pans out to the end of his front walk by the road and fill them with cold water from his well. Then he would bring out the two pails of milk and place them in the pans. He would cover them with a dish towel. I would stop on the way to the creamery with our milk and empty Mr. Haines' pails into our cans. It was always there, early in the morning. I never had to wait once. At the end of the month, Mr. Haynes would give my father the number of quarts of milk he had and my father would pay him.

Also, during the year, there was a small income from the farm. There were a few gallons of maple syrup to sell in the spring and possibly a few bushels of potatoes or cords of wood which would bring in a little money, and, together with the money from the milk would help to pay the taxes, insurance and other little bills. Hopefully there would be a few dollars left over at the end of the year.

Mr. Haynes was a good neighbor—understanding and sympathetic. His few apple trees bore delicious fruit which he shared with us.

Once while trying to get a skunk from under his barn which I had caught in a trap, I was sprayed in the face by its stinging, foul smelling essence. I was blinded and shouted for help. Mr. Haynes came, washed my face and eyes with warm water and soap so I could see to get home.

Mr. Haynes was a faithful church member. Every Sunday, he could be seen walking down the street to the Methodist Church. He always wore his black suit, a little black felt hat with turned up brim and carried an umbrella or overcoat as the weather required. Even after he became stone deaf, he was always in his church pew on Sunday. As he became older, he developed a mild intestinal problem. The frequent escape and explosion of trapped gas as Mr. Haynes slowly plodded along cause a rather loud intermittent report which he was probably unaware of and never heard, but which brought a quiet smile to those nearby.

Then, too, Mr. Haynes occasionally forgot which day of the week Sunday was on. Several times he was seen walking to church on a Saturday in his Sunday best. Another time he took a leather harness to John Irish, the local shoemaker, to be repaired on a Sunday morning.

The Hayneses had no social life. I never heard of anyone ever visiting them or of their ever calling on any friend or neighbor. They were never seen at a church supper or community picnic or other social occasion. Mrs. Haynes was seldom seen outside her house. They had no telephone.

After Mrs. Haynes' death, his sister, Mary Haynes, came to keep house for Mr. Haynes. She was a refined, educated nurse. For several years, at Christmas time, she and Mr. Haynes gave me a subscription to The American Magazine and also a box of chocolate candy.

Mr. Haynes died in the hay field, at work with his boots on. He was discovered dead on the ground by Calvin, who had come late in the afternoon to help draw a load of hay. Mary was notified and came to the field with bottles of medicine, but it was too late. He was gone—a frail little old man who had worked and saved all his life. The farm was paid for and he had six thousand dollars in the bank.

THE LEMUEL HITCHCOCK FAMILY

Of the ten children of Deacon Lemuel Hitchcock, the first settler to Big Hollow in 1795, three sons grew up and remained in the valley. They married and had large families: Lucius had six children; Deacon Lemuel II, seven, and Zalmon, nine. Zalmon's family died out with the death of Austin in 1959. Lucius' descendants increased and remained in the valley through the third generation, but most of his great-grandchildren moved away or died, with the exception of Wilfred Hitchcock, William's youngest son, who remained in the valley with two of his sons, James and Dennis, and their families; and Edwin's daughter, Judy Hitchcock Cook, and two children.

The descendants of Deacon Lemuel II, however, remained in Big Hollow and had children. Lemuel Hitchcock, the third-generation descendant of the original Deacon Lemuel, and his wife Sarah Phelps Hitchcock had four sons and four daughters, all of whom lived in big Hollow all their lives. Leonard died as a young man. Charlie never married. Anson and George both married but had no children. Frankie married Henry Osborn and had one son, Raymond; Dell married Eugene Lewis and had Alice, Ethel and Leon. Jessie married Will Vining and had Leonard, Viola and Lemuel. Minnie married Charlie Baker and had one son, Walter. She later married Frank Palmer.

Lemuel and Sarah's eight grandchildren and ten great-grandchildren remained in Maplecrest and raised their families there. At present, in 1993, there are approximately 60 descendants of Lemuel and Sarah Phelps Hitchcock living in or near Maplecrest. The descendants of Lemuel Hitchcock constitute the strong core of the Maplecrest Free Methodist Church, one of the largest and strongest churches, spiritually and financially, in Greene County. The present pastor of the church is the Rev. James Shields, who recently followed the Rev. Donald Baker, a member of the seventh generation of the original Deacon Lemuel Hitchcock.

The four daughters of Lemuel and Sarah, Frankie, Jessie, Dell and Minnie, and their descendants exerted a tremendous economic and spiritual influence on Maplecrest village and the big basin at the eastern end of the Windham valley during the twentieth century.

During the second and third decades of the century, with the railroad coming into the mountains, the big hotels and other resorts did a thriving business in the summer months. Chicken dealers in Maplecrest, Will Vining, Eugene Lewis and Walter Bray, bought and sold thousands of chickens along with eggs and butter. These same dealers, together with Ray Osborn, handled quantities of maple syrup and maple sugar, which they purchased each year from local farmers and sold in river-town communities.

While World War II was in progress and for some time after, Vining Brothers, in their enormous chicken houses, raised thousands of chickens to help feed the hungry population. In more recent years, Ray Osborn started and established a large John Deere dealership which brought farmers and lumbermen from far and near to make purchases and have repairs made. More recently still, Kenneth Stewart, Sr. and his son, Ken, have built a large G.M.C. truck dealership which has been so successful over the years that national awards have been made to the dealership for their sales and repair records.

For many years, Ken Stewart, Sr. did a thriving business in supplying businesses, resorts and private homes with fresh vegetables, fruit and fish which he secured from the Albany Farmers' Market.

Lemuel Vining (fifth generation) and his son Lemuel and two grandsons for many years were in the hay business. To buy hay, they would often go to the western part of the state and as far north as the Adirondacks. The market for the hay might be as far away as Long Island, Connecticut or Massachusetts.

Maplecrest is not an ideal business location as it is a dead-end valley, with no outlet other than the entrance at the western end over the bridge by the post office. State Route 23, connecting with the Thruway and other important highways, is five miles away. The only other road out of the valley is County Route 40, which is steep and crooked and leads to East Jewett and Tannersville.

Dell and Gene Lewis lived in a nice old house in the middle of the village on the left side of the street, just below Dell's parents' home. There was a large garden space between the two houses with a white picket fence in front and a nice walk shaded by large maple trees.

Gene was a short, stout, rather quiet and independent businessman. It was said that he had been a stonemason in his earlier days. Before his death, he built a stone pier at his driveway entrance. Gene was a loving father of his children, especially his only son, Leon.

Leon had about everything he wanted—nice clothes, too much delicious food which made him fat like his father—and was allowed to do anything he wanted to do. His father bought him a nice billy goat with horns, a harness and a miniature brightly painted farm wagon. Leon enjoyed driving his goat with his whip and little wagon up and down the street. The neighbors pitied the poor goat.

Several incidents happened at school which showed Leon's aggressive attitude. Once when we were choosing teams to play ball during the noon recess, all the boys but Leon had been chosen for one side or the other. Although it was the other captain's turn to choose, he shouted, "I don't want Leon." As the second captain, I stood silently wondering what was going to happen next when Leon suddenly jumped on me, knocked me to the ground and started pummeling me with his fists. In desperation, I took Leon on my side.

I recall another occasion when Leon had some difference with several of us boys. At the close of school in the afternoon, he ran ahead of all of us, collected a pile of stones on the bridge by the post office and wouldn't let any of us cross. I had to walk all the way home through the brush on the opposite side of the creek back of the village and finally cross over the creek on the Slater Road bridge near my home.

The teachers often had trouble disciplining Leon. Raymond Moseman, an excellent teacher and a refined Christian gentleman was, one day at his wit's end, and shook Leon up. And in so doing he tore Leon's sweater. Dell and Gene were furious and required Raymond to buy Leon a new one.

Blanche Miller, another superior teacher, drove her horse and wagon from her home on the Old Road near Windham to school each day. She kept the horse in George Rickard's barn just above the school. Often, in the morning, she would stop at the school to bring in her books and lunch rather than carry them back from the barn. One morning while Blanche was in the schoolhouse, Leon climbed on the horse's back and insisted on riding it up to the barn. Blanche silently deliberated for a moment, then got into her wagon behind the horse with Leon on its back and drove as best she could up to the barn.

One year, Lemmie, Leon and I decided to go into the maple syrup business together. We took boards from my father's lumber pile and built a sap house across the creek up in the pasture lot where the maple trees were. We also built a small stone arch for a syrup pan and had a stove pipe extending up through the roof. With about 25 buckets hanging on the trees, we were ready to produce maple syrup. Following the first "good run of sap," Lemmie and I sat in the sap house in front of the fire watching the sap boil in the pan. Suddenly, the little shack filled with smoke. Choking, Lemmie and I staggered to the outside. Leon had climbed up on the roof, stuffed the stove pipe full of leaves and pine needles and had then gone home. That little episode ended the maple syrup making for that season.

Leon grew up to be a friendly, hard-working man. During the last years of his life, he and my brother Edwin worked together at the Peckham Stone Crusher in Catskill.

Dell and Gene's daughter, Alice, married Vernon Van and they had two daughters. Later, they purchased a boarding house in Windham and for many years operated it successfully. After Vernon died, Alice married his brother, Claude Van.

Ethel, the other daughter, married Vance Fancher and they had several children. Leonard built up the Victory Oldsmobile garage business in Hensonville, which became one of the leading car dealerships in Greene County. His brother, Richard, a soldier in World War II, was killed in action near the close of the war, on one of the South Pacific Islands around 1945. A Nature Lodge building at the Rip Van Winkle Boy Scout Council's Camp TriMount was built and dedicated to his memory.

Gene and Will Vining operated a second grocery store for several years in Maplecrest across from the Sugar Maples dining hall. For most of his life, Gene was a chicken dealer and died in middle age.

Dell was a good housekeeper, cook and a hospitable hostess with lots of time for visitors. Her home was a social center with good neighbors nearby, such as Mose and Hat Hitchcock across the street; John and Emma Phelps, her mother and father, a stone's throw away; and her sister Minnie a regular caller. There were also many other village neighbors who, during the boarding season in the summers, would gather on her porch to visit with Sugar Maples guests who had been coming to the famous resort for many years. They had become acquainted with Dell and spent many a pleasant afternoon on her front porch as did her other good friends, Mary Gray and Mrs. Philips.

Dell and her children were regular attendants at the Free Methodist Church as long as the children were small and remained at home.

Frankie Hitchcock Osborn and husband Henry lived in the little house across the brook just above the old Free Methodist Church. There were 10 to 15 acres to the little farm. Henry usually had two cows, some chickens and a pig or two, which he cared for while working for local farmers. Henry was a pleasant, agreeable man. He often worked for us by the day. Mornings, he would drive his two cows up the road, across the bridge and up the hill to his pasture. Then he would walk down the hill, cross the bridge and come up the road to our farm where he worked all day for about two dollars in wages. Frankie and Henry had only one son, Ray, who grew up and made great contributions to the community.

Frankie for more than 50 years was a faithful and dedicated member of the Free Methodist Church. She was not one of the original members in 1871, but in later years when many of the older members had died and the little church was struggling to survive, it was Frankie, Emma Phelps and Mrs. John Moseman who helped keep the church alive with their sacrificial giving, hard work and regular attendance. Frankie was a remarkable woman who exerted a stable and strong Christian influence in her church and in the Big Hollow community.

MINNIE HITCHCOCK BAKER PALMER

Minnie, a few years after her marriage to Charlie Baker, found herself alone with a son, Walter, to support and bring up. Sometime later she married Frank Palmer. Frank was an energetic and industrious workman. He was in great demand for wallpapering. He did the papering and Minnie, the pasting. They made a productive team, doing quality work fast and for a reasonable fee. Frank also did painting and barbering for twenty-five cents a haircut. Over the years, they lived at several locations in the little village: in Carrie Van's old house across from the cemetery, in Lem and Sate's house, in a clubhouse on Manley Mallory's property, and in a new house below the Free Methodist Church where Pete and Freda Peck now live.

Minnie kept her house clean and attractive. She and Frank were early risers and, since she didn't have as much work as her sisters, she would start out early in the morning to visit her sisters Jessie, Dell, Mother Sate and brother Charlie, and on to sister Frankie's; at least once a week she also would walk up to brother George's and on up the Slater Road to spend some time with brother Anson and wife. Minnie's visits and the local telephone line kept the family members together in a close, attached fellowship as long as they lived. The Lem Hitchcock descendants became the heart of the Free Methodist Church and the community for many years.

Meanwhile, Walter grew up and worked for Ray Osborn for many years. Later, he married Dorothy Vining of Hensonville and over the years they had five children—Donald, Harold, Clifford, Jere and Jean.

For a number of years, Walter owned and operated a black fox breeding farm and later secured employment with the New York State Conservation Department where he worked until his retirement.

Donald became a Free Methodist minister and retired as the pastor of the Maplecrest Free Methodist Church. Harold, for several years, owned and operated a John Deere lawn mower and snowmobile dealership in Hensonville. Later, he operated a tractor repair shop in Maplecrest; and is now working for a large John Deere dealer in the Albany area. Jere, also a mechanic, is working in Prattsville. At one time, the three brothers and their families were all living in Maplecrest.

Clifford became a school teacher and then a school superintendent. For many years he worked in schools in the Adirondacks. Now, he and his family are in Corpus Christi, Texas, where he is teaching and plans to retire soon.

Jean Baker Bechple worked for sometime with the Free Methodist Publishing House and is now an executive secretary to the president of Kansas City College, Kansas City, Kansas.

Dorothy died in 1986, but Walter, at 90 years of age, is healthy and strong. He lives alone in his Maplecrest home. Minnie's son, grandchildren and their families are contributing members of our great American society and a great asset to the Maplecrest Valley.

JESSIE AND WILL VINING

Jessie and Will's first home, where their three children were born, was at the upper end of the village across from the cemetery. This house burned and they moved to what was then known as the Lydia DuBois home across from the Sugar Maples office, where Mr. and Mrs. Fuller, owners of Sugar Maples, now live.

Jessie was a "born again" Christian and lived a Christian life—bringing up her children as Christians was an important part of her life. At an early age, the children learned to study the Bible, memorize scripture passages, pray and attend church services regularly.

As a young girl, Jessie had formed a close friendship with Inez Mallory, who later married Charles Phelps. Inez, too, was a dedicated Christian. Jessie, Inez, and Frankie Osborn, together with John Howard, the VanValin family and several others became a strong and united team in establishing the Free Methodist Church and in helping it to grow under the deep spiritual leadership of strong fundamental preachers of the gospel.

Leonard, the older son of Jessie and Will, became a druggist, but after a short time left that career because of ill health. He returned to Big Hollow as a businessman following in the steps of his father and members of his mother's family. Leonard and Lemuel formed a partnership, purchased the John Haynes farm and started raising chickens.

In 1924, Leonard had married Louise Chatfield of Maplecrest and they had three sons—Leonard Jr., Burdette and Gilbert. Leonard had several tragic experiences during his lifetime. In 1938, a disastrous early morning fire destroyed their home and took Louise's life while she attempted to rescue her sons. In 1939 he married Marguerite Frasier of Allaben and they had two sons, Wesley and David. Then, in 1955, a fatal accident took the life of their son David and his cousin Donald DeHoff as the boys were riding a tractor down Slater Road, returning from a trip to pick blackberries. And in 1963, Leonard's son Burdette became a victim of sugar diabetes and died, leaving a widow and three children. Finally, in 1976, Leonard himself died of cancer.

During Leonard's lifetime he had established a reputation of being a strong, dedicated Christian and a capable businessman. His memory lives on.

Viola, Jessie and Will's daughter, was a natural born poet and teacher. She was a leader in the church and Sunday school for many years. Viola and Arbreta Phelps became close friends as their mothers were. Viola married Kenneth Stewart who had come to Big Hollow from Westerlo to find employment. Viola and Kenneth had three children: Kenneth, Jr., who became a partner in business with his father and later took over the G.M.C. truck agency in Maplecrest; Janet who married a minister of the Free Methodist Church who became a District Superintendent of the Genesee Conference and later a bishop; and Larry, who became a school teacher and for many years has been principal of a Catskill Village school.

Viola was a devoted daughter, living near her parents in Maplecrest. She and her mother Jessie had a close relationship during Jessie's last years and they enjoyed much time together. Viola died in 1964 at the age of 59.

Lemuel, the youngest of Jessie and Will's children, has spent his entire life as a Maplecrest resident. He married Thelma Swanker from a place near Schenectady and they had one son Lemuel Jr., a seventh-generation descendant of Deacon Lemuel and the fifth generation to bear the name Lemuel.

Following Leonard's death, Lemuel and his son Lemuel, Jr. were in business together for a number of years, raising and selling chickens and dealing in hay, straw and mulch for banking newly constructed highways. Lemuel Jr. married Jody Tessaro, daughter of Evangelist Rev. A.R. Tessaro, and they had four children: Debra, Denise, Frederick and Jeffrey. As the sons of Lemuel Jr. grew older, they went into the hay business with their father, driving trucks and tractor trailers long distances to buy hay for cows and horses.

Lemuel Sr. retired. He and Thelma had built a brick house at the upper end of the flat of the John Haynes farm. This was the first and only brick house ever built in Maplecrest, a beautiful building. When Thelma died in 1976, Lemuel Sr. married his brother Leonard's widow, Marguerite Frasier Vining, in 1977. He then moved into the home of Marguerite and Leonard, which is on an elevation overlooking the upper end of the village, the first Free Methodist Church building and the homes where he worked most of his life.

In the 1980's there was a building boom in the Catskill Mountains. The ski slopes at Hunter and Windham attracted many people to the area from New York City, about two hours away. Many of these people admired the beauty and grandeur of the mountains, and some began purchasing land and erecting new homes. Local carpenters and contractors went into the construction business. Several housing developments sprang up near the ski slopes and in neighboring areas.

Fred and Jeff Vining were quick to see new opportunities for business and began a housing development on the hill at the end of Slater Road. Several new houses were erected by the brothers, who did nearly all the labor of construction.

Lemuel Sr., is now retired. He and his family have been faithful, dedicated members of the Free Methodist Church since childhood. They have seen the congregation grow from a small group to one of the largest in Greene County.

THE GRAYS AND VANS

Archie and Mary Gray and Archie's brother Richard were of Irish descent. They lived summers in the house directly across from the cemetery. Winters they lived in New York City doing housekeeping work in the large hotels.

Mary was a cheerful, likeable lady, a dear and close friend of Lem's four daughters and their families. She attended the Free Methodist Church and was a pleasant addition to the village.

Archie, her husband, was a nervous, active man with flashing black eyes. He considered himself a skilled electrician. At a local Big Hollow telephone meeting in the schoolhouse one evening, he tried to persuade the group to run another telephone line up through the valley, making it unnecessary for every home to have its own ground wire. It probably was a good idea, but Archie's fast talk, his enthusiasm and excitement together with his blackboard illustrations were so amusing that there was no action taken on his proposal. It was also generally believed that Archie's attempt to repair the plumbing and electrical systems in the Vining Brother's home resulted in the house burning to the ground. Archie and Richard were recognized as good furniture upholsterers and they did considerable upholstery work in the barn at the rear of their property.

Richard, a bachelor, was a quiet, scholarly appearing person. Mornings, he walked down through the village to the post office to get his New York Herald Tribune, which he read religiously. He considered himself an authority on all current topics. Seeing Richard walking briskly down the street, carefully dressed and puffing away contentedly on his straight stem pipe, was a pleasant and enjoyable sight. The natives admired Richard and were awed at his knowledge, although we seldom knew what he was talking about. We listened to him as he was a talker and not a conversationalist. Busy people avoided him, as so much time was taken in his detailed explanation of a matter. Richard had a large productive garden each summer and Mary prepared many cans of vegetables and fruit for winter use in their city home.

The Grays were instrumental in attracting some of their city friends to move to the country to live—the Dormans, Straussers, Rappleyeas, Sallies and Gribbonses were among friends who bought homes in or near Maplecrest and came here to live. The three Grays made life in the little community somewhat more enjoyable and exciting.

Carrie Van and her four children—George, Sigsbee, Lena and Grace—lived in probably the oldest house in the village, next to the Grays and directly across from the cemetery. It was a weather-beaten and neglected, two-family house.

Mrs. Van was a good woman, quiet and hard-working. She managed to keep her family together by taking in washings and working for neighbors, often at a dollar a day. The children, as they grew older, earned a little money doing odd jobs and running errands.

George became a soldier in World War I and served overseas in France. He brought home fanciful tales of battlefield scenes. With his army pay, he bought a turkey for his mother and family one Thanksgiving. Turkey, at that time, was a great rarity and the first taste we ever had of turkey meat was a portion Mrs. Van sent up to our family.

Sigsbee worked for local farmers, then went to the Manorkill area where he married, bought a home and worked in a creamery for many years.

Grace remained home with her mother as long as she lived and then spent the rest of her days with her sister Lena and family in Windham. Lena worked for local housewives for several years and married Maurice Benjamin, a carpenter and contractor, in Windham. They had one daughter, Birdie, who grew up and married Douglas Goff, a local barber.

E.M. HITCHCOCK, THE LAW AND
BRAY FAMILIES

E.M. Hitchcock, commonly known as "Mose," was the Big Hollow blacksmith for decades. Mose put new shoes on horses and oxen; shaped iron in his old forge for braces and hinges on doors and wagons; and drilled holes in iron with his big hand-operated drill press. Moreover, Mose's blacksmith shop served as the social center for retired men, those well-to-do, and the ill and disabled. The shop was in a perfect location across from the post office and store and at the junction of three roads—Main Street, the East Jewett and the Hensonville roads. It was easy to see anyone going to the store and post office or, on the other hand, those entering or leaving Big Hollow.

Anyone sitting in the big doorway of the shop whittling or chewing on the stub of an old cigar could merely by lifting his eyes, detect the movement of a person, speculate as to what he was up to, and, after a moment of silent meditation, make a wise statement which in turn could excite the attention of the other old cronies, resulting in a lengthy discussion ending up with a brief evaluation of the person's life and his lot in life.

During the summer months, the little village was flooded with several hundred city guests at Sugar Maples, who would stroll by the old shop on their way to the store and post office. This made eye-viewing more interesting and enjoyable. The boarders would take a look at the old fellows in the doorway of the shop and then peer into the dark old place. There they would see Mose sitting in an old broken chair tipping back against the wall, swatting flies as they chanced to land on his dirty old leather apron.

Mose was a happy, easy-going man who never complained about life and enjoyed conversing with people. He was witty and had a sense of humor. Afternoons, he often closed his shop early and went fishing as he was a skilled fly fisherman and easily caught his limit of trout in the Batavia Kill.

Somehow, Mose and Hat had become acquainted with several city boarders and their families, by the name of Miller. These families boarded with Mose and Hat for several summers. The brothers were big New York City dealers in pork and had a large slaughter house. One summer they purchased enough hogs and pigs on the Mountain Top to ship a carload from the railroad station in Hunter to their New York City plant.

Summers, Mose bought cakes of ice from me for his ice box. I would climb up in our ice house, loosen a cake of ice, throw it to the ground, wash it free of sawdust, hitch up the horse and take it down in the village to Mose's house. There I would carry it into his kitchen and carefully place it in the ice box. Mose paid me a quarter each week for supplying him with ice. He also introduced me to Mr. and Mrs. Charles Ising, city people who owned a bungalow at the top of the Big Hollow Mountain about two miles from our farm. I supplied them with ice for a number of summers for a dollar a week. Thus, I made a little money during the summer months. My father didn't demand pay for the ice as I worked full time for him for no pay.

Mose and Hat had only one child, a son Harold, whom they loved dearly. Harold was tall and slim, a scholarly looking fellow, rather quiet, and a good ball player. He was the first person I ever saw fishing on Sunday, and I was shocked. Hat had two sisters and a brother, Cyrus Tibbals of Windham, the local undertaker. None of them had any children and so Harold was the only descendant of the four Tibbals families.

Harold taught school for a while, but didn't care for it. His Uncle Cy encouraged him to go to a mortician's school and become an undertaker. He returned home and went into business with his Uncle Cy in Windham, but that didn't appeal to him either. Finally, he ended up in Ilion, New York, working for the Remington Rand Typewriter Company.

Meanwhile, Harold had met and married a beautiful blond by the name of Beatrice. They had their home in Ilion and had one son. Harold played first clarinet in the Remington Rand Band, which became quite well-known and gave concerts in many cities. Mose was very proud of his only son. After receiving a letter from him, he would report at the shop on Harold's latest musical experience, which, he pointed out, was all on company time with all tour expenses paid.

Occasionally, in the summer, Harold and his family visited his parents in Maplecrest. On one of these visits, Hat and Bea went for a walk while the supper was cooking. When they returned, a dish Bea prepared had burned. Hat spoke a bit quickly about the matter which angered Bea. She never came to Maplecrest again. Hat wrote letter after letter apologizing, begging forgiveness and expressing her grief and sorrow, but she never saw Bea again. When Harold came to visit his parents, Bea would stop off and stay with friends in Windham.

As the years passed, the automobile and tractor replaced the horse. Mose closed his shop, sold it to Sugar Maples and retired. Hat died. Mose, now an old man, sold his home and went to Ilion to pass his last days with Harold and Bea.

Once, when my parents were visiting us in Dolgeville, we decided to go to Utica shopping and for a ride through the beautiful Mohawk Valley. On the way home, we stopped in Ilion to see our old friend and neighbor, Mose. Harold lived on a steep street coming up out of the valley. Mose was not at home. We were told that he was probably up on the hill at the end of the street where he often went for a walk in the large field. At first we saw no one, then off at a distance we saw an old man with a cane shuffling toward us. It was Mose. We had a good visit with him, but we never saw him again.

THE LAWS

Raymond Moseman and family lived in the house below Mose's, with Aunt Mary and Aunt Charlotte living upstairs. The next property was that of Romaine Law.

Romaine and Fannie Drum Law, his wife, and four children Julia, Nellie, Bernard and Arthur, lived in the new house Romaine had built. During Romaine's lifetime, he showed his versatility in several ways. He was the local merchant, postmaster, Methodist Church organist and Sunday school teacher, carpenter, farmer, and for many years, a stonemason who built stone walls and stone decorations for the Sugar Maples Resort.

Romaine was slim and of medium height, with black eyes, black hair and a black mustache. He was a quiet, friendly man. After living in the street for sometime, the family moved to the Batavia Kill Farm below the village where he operated the farm and continued with the store and postmaster work. Later, he and Fannie moved into a small house below Windham village. The four children grew up, married and moved away to distant homes, with the exception of Nellie, who married Ernest Barnum and settled in Prattsville.

THE BRAYS

Walter and Claudia Bray had one daughter, Alda. She grew up, earned good marks in school and gave piano lessons. She was popular among her friends.

On a small piece of property on the street between the Law home and Dorland Peck's home, which Walter had bought, the Brays built a new house and barn. Walter was a businessman dealing in maple syrup and sugar, potatoes and for some time was a partner with Will Vining in the chicken business.

Claudia was very religious, but fickle, talkative, proud and a complainer. At one time or another, she was a faithful member and leader in each of the churches, then something would happen and she would leave for one of the other churches. She was proud of herself and her knowledge, her new home, her husband's business ability and her daughter's popularity and achievements.

One story has it that Claudia once angrily told a neighbor that if he were her husband she would want to die, and he replied, "If you were my wife, I would want to die." Claudia was seldom well. She was a hypochondriac, always imagining she had some illness.

While Alda was in high school, Claudie came to believe she needed a hired girl to help with the house work. A rather attractive young lady by the name of Pearl Waterman was hired. In time, Walter and Pearl fell in love and ran away together, leaving Claudie and Alda alone. It was a terrible tragedy in those days.

As the Sugar Maples Resort business prospered and grew, Gus Moseman, the proprietor, bought more and more village property. He finally secured the former Law house and the Peck house on either side of the Bray home. Then, Gus and Claudie had a dispute and in anger he built a 10 ft. high unpainted board fence each side of the Bray house extending from the road to the back of the house. This "spite fence" was up for several years—a reflection on the families involved and the little community as well.

Alda and Claudie left Maplecrest and moved to Kenmore near Buffalo, where Alda secured employment. She married twice and had a son. Alda kept her mother with her and took care of her as long as she lived.

Over the years, friends corresponded with Alda and invited her to come for a visit, but she never returned to Big Hollow. She died February 1, 1980 at the age of 71.

THE MOSEMANS: WILLIAM HENRY, JOHN, AND RAYMOND

It is believed that the Birdsell Moseman family came to Big Hollow around the year 1850 from Halcott Center, a far-distant settlement in Greene County near Fleischmanns in Delaware County. Birdsell had three sons—Robert, William Henry and John. Robert married Jennie Calhoun of Durham, a woman of forceful character and civic spirit. They had one son, Sherwood A. Moseman, born April 20, 1883. Robert died at a young age and his widow, Jennie, married her brother-in-law William Henry.

William Henry was a short, slim man, quiet and retiring. He and his brother Robert had opened the grocery store in Big Hollow. After Robert's death, William Henry operated the store and in 1879 was appointed postmaster. The Big Hollow post office had opened in 1829.

For some years, Sherwood (Gus) operated the store with his step-father. Later on Gus took over the store and became the postmaster in 1905 and again in 1918, for a total of 15 years. In 1925, he sold the store to Valentine W. Morrow, who operated it and served as postmaster for 40 years.

Following Jennie's death in 1918 in the great influenza epidemic which swept the country, William Henry retired to a quite, withdrawn life in his home across from the store.

About this time, Gus and his wife Adelaide (Newkirk) and family had returned to Big Hollow from Staten Island and took over the store and post office. His second daughter Bertha was just about my age. She was a beautiful city girl—talented, musical and popular. Bertha was a newcomer to the community and to the one-room school. We were both in the sixth grade. Raymond Moseman was the teacher. There were around 20 of us in the eight grades of the school including her sisters Fredonia and Vernette and my brother Edwin and sister Eva.

Bertha was quiet, ladylike, friendly and an excellent pupil. I was a farmer's son, shy, timid, with a painful inferiority complex, a mediocre learner, and terribly ill at ease in the presence of girls, in whom I was not particularly interested. Bertha liked the boys and was popular with them. She would ride down the hill with Lemmie Vining and his cousin Alfred and walk back up the hill with them, occasionally glancing longingly at me. Stupid me. I would look away, yet be pleased that she had noticed me.

Love is strange and indescribable. Poor, wonderful, beautiful Bertha. She fell so madly in love with me. She couldn't seem to give me up. Her wild, mad infatuation for me continued through high school until circumstances separated us. During this time, church activities brought us together in a comfortable, natural way. My mother taught the young people's Sunday school class of which we both were members. Her father was church choir director and we both sang in the choir. Then, too, our parents were pleased that we seemed drawn to each other. Gus' mother, Jennie, had wanted him to marry my mother Grace, as I heard my mother mention several times, and Gus seemed to take a liking to me.

While I was janitor of the Presbyterian church, where I was paid a small sum to start two wood-stove fires, sweep, dust and arrange the books orderly in the pew racks, I would get to the church early to shovel the paths and get the church warm for services. Bertha, who lived down the street just a little way, would walk up early, too. We would be together alone for at least half an hour before anyone else arrived. I suppose she was happy just to be in the presence of her dear friend, and I was pleased to have her there, but I generally busied myself so with my mediocre job that I didn't have a second to chat with her or even to look at her.

The mid-week prayer meeting at the private homes afforded a convenient opportunity for Bertha and me to be together. Often I would be the only boy there with a car. After the meeting, of course, there usually were one or two with no way home. Bertha would sit next to me and when it was good sledding on the mountain, we would walk to the top of the mountain, sit on the sled and talk together for a while before riding down to the village and then walking back up again. One night, I remember, a snow storm was raging and we sat at the top of the mountain holding hands, covered with snow.

The winter of 1922-23 was long remembered for a great amount of snow. Roads were unplowed. Travel was only with horses and sleighs. It was my first year in Windham High School and I drove our horses and sleigh to Windham for 62 days, picking up students along the way and bringing them home at night.

After leaving Hensonville, there would be only a few left in the sleigh—Fredonia, Alda Bray and one or two others. We sat on hay in the sleigh box with horse blankets over us. The horses were always in a hurry to get home and needed no guidance, but I sat at the front with Bertha alone behind me, instead of beside me.

As William Henry grew older, he stayed by himself most of the time. He hung a quart pail on a maple tree for me to fill mornings with milk as I drove to the creamery. I began receiving letters in the milk pail addressed to Knight Elwood and signed by Princess Elizabeth. They were charming, imaginative letters of a beautiful princess Bertha corresponding with her beloved knight.

The Sugar Maples Resort was growing rapidly as Gus dreamed and saw visions of a great and beautiful hotel in the Catskills. Addie and the three daughters worked long days during the summer months. Then early in the fall they would all leave to spend the winter months in Florida. Bertha and Fredonia were taken out of high school before graduation.

I continued in high school and graduated in 1927. The following year I went to Delhi Teachers Training Class with four of my classmates and began my teaching career. Bertha and I were separated for the rest of our lives. Occasionally, I saw her on the sidewalk during the summer months. I heard she kept company with John Martin, Gus' partner, for a while. Then she married Richard Veith, a very pleasant fellow, but an alcoholic. They had one son, Dickie. Later, they separated. Finally, she had a happy marriage with Raymond Lewis, an associate at Sugar Maples. They had one son, Ray, Jr. This marriage lasted until Bertha died in 1989.

I recall vividly that young girl-boy school romance. I hope and pray that God and Bertha have forgiven me for my rudeness and cruelty to a very wonderful person and friend.

John Moseman was a serious, stern man. He always had money to lend and took mortgages on farms and other property. He was a carpenter by trade, but never seemed to be too occupied with work. John and his wife, Mattie, a devout Free Methodist, had two children, Raymond and Pearl. She married Hervey Smith, a hay dealer in Pennsylvania. They had no children.

Raymond married Blanche Truesdell of Beachers Corners and they had four children—Birdsell, Gerald, Eleanor and Edith. They all grew up in Big Hollow, married and moved away. Birdsell became a teacher like his father.

Raymond was a fine Christian, public-spirited man. He taught in one-room schools for a few years and then secured a position in the Windham School where he taught until his death.

He and his family were dedicated members of the Free Methodist Church where he served as Sunday school superintendent and teacher. He assisted Val Morrow with the organization of a Boy Scout Troop in the village. Raymond died suddenly in middle age. Blanche later remarried and moved to Oneonta.

John's first wife died and he remarried. They lived in Maplecrest until both died. Shortly after, the Sugar Maples Resort closed. There was not a single person living in Maplecrest by the name of Moseman. An important family was gone with the exception of Bertha's husband Raymond Lewis, their son Raymond, Jr. and two sons Kim and Mark Lewis of Raymond, Jr. and Lorie Gribbons.

PEOPLE ON THE MOUNTAIN ROAD

The John Irish home was the first place up the Mountain Road on the right. John was a cobbler who repaired shoes and harnesses. He was tall and slim. His bench was by a window looking down the street in front of the store. Josephine, his wife, was a little woman. She taught the adult ladies class in the Presbyterian Sunday school for many years.

The Irish family had once lived on the Davis farm on the Ridge Road to East Windham. Their three sons, Lewis, George and David, had walked the mile down the road to the school house near the Chatfield home. Later, they disposed of the farm and moved to the village property.

At one time when Gus Moseman was operating his store, he attended a revival meeting at the Free Methodist Church and was converted. He immediately threw all his tobacco products from the store into the creek.

Realizing there was a demand for tobacco, Mrs. Irish put a supply in her front room, behind John's cobbler's bench. Soon, she added a small showcase of penny and nickel candies. She also began baking big delicious loaves of bread and selling them for ten cents a loaf. She was in business.

The Irishes' front room was a warm, comfortable place to visit. Josie was a lovable little lady and John was a pleasant, agreeable cobbler. It was a welcome place to pause for a chat.

In time John and Josie became elderly people. John was ill for a long time before he died. Local people explained that he lingered on because he had so much vitality, but no one seemed to know what vitality was.

After John and Josie were gone, their youngest son, David, and his wife, Lucy Crandell Irish, purchased the place and lived there for many years with their two daughters, Doris and Barbara. David was a carpenter and for many years worked at Sugar Maples as caretaker during the winter months.

Across the road from the Irish home, Manly Mallory built a new house. It, too, commanded a nice view of the triangle at the front of the store. Manly and his wife Nelia lived here for many years until she became sick and died. And it remained his home until he died many years later. When Gus and his family returned to Big Hollow from Staten Island, the house must have been vacant because they rented it for several months. It was while the Mosemans lived here that Gus broke his leg and was laid up for several weeks.

For at least twenty years, there was no other dwelling above the Mallory home on the left side of the road. On the right side, however, Henry Vining, a bachelor, built a small, three-room house just above the Irishes'. Henry was quick tempered, quite deaf, and had a wooden leg, which Henry Slater had made for him. He was a carpenter and after Mr. Irish's death, took over his shoe and harness business.

A short distance on up the road was the small farm of Charlie and Frankie Garvey. Frankie, Charlie's second wife, was an epileptic and had frequent seizures, making it almost impossible for her to do her housework and care for their two children, Edwin and Lydia. Charlie, a little man, tried to run his farm, take care of Frankie, do the housework and care for the children. He did as well as was possible for him.

After Frankie died, Lydia spent some time in an orphanage, later married and moved to the northern part of the State. Edwin grew up and became a skilled car mechanic and welder. He operated the Maplecrest garage with Edwin Hitchcock and later with his son Ronny who was an excellent mechanic and welder.

Charlie Garvey's first wife was a crippled girl, Kathy Ham, whom he abducted one night by taking her out of her bedroom window, according to local lore. They were married and had two children, Martin Garvey, who married Mina DeLong Winchell, a widow; and Anna, who married Ashley Hoyt and had a large family. They all lived on a farm between Maplecrest and Hensonville.

On the second sharp curve on the mountain road above the Garvey farm, the Barnum-DeLong road branched off to the left. On this road lived the Reuben and Lydia Tompkins DeLong family with their nine children—Mary, Frances, Mina, Rose, Pearl, Joseph, Calvin, Vernon and Merritt. Pearl, the youngest, eloped with and married John Ruoff, a much older man, and died before the birth of their first child.

A short distance beyond Mr. DeLong's small farm and little house with its single outside door was the farm of Martin and Carrie Barnum. The two farms were on a plateau at the western end of the Black Head-Black Dome range. The Barnums' four children were Albert, who was born blind; Raymond, an epileptic; Elmer, who would talk only with the immediate members of his family; and Flora, who became ill and died at the age of 12.

Also on this road was an abandoned farm once owned by a Hitchcock and later his son-in-law, Thurston Moore of Hensonville. To this abandoned farm moved Abe and Hattie Miles Williams and their six children—Ida, Hilda, Emma, Charlie, Dan and Myron. So, over the years, there were nearly 20 children at one time or another walking down the long mountain road to the little one-room school house below the post office and bridge. In the early days, the Barnum-DeLong road followed along the south side of the Black Head-Black Dome range all the way up the East Jewett Valley to the Colgate farm. An early map indicates there were several houses on this road far up on the side of the mountain above the Eastkill Valley.

On the main Mountain road just opposite the Barnum Road turn was a small plateau large enough for a little meadow, garden, barn and house. Here, Charlie and Orrie Joselyn Haddon lived. Charlie was a small, quiet, soft-spoken man. Orrie was a man-hater—sullen, stern and hostile to Charlie. She was a meticulous housekeeper and would not allow Charlie to enter the house with his shoes or boots on. There were only certain places he could walk in the house and only certain chairs he could sit in. A city lady who had observed Mrs. Haddon's behavior came to believe she was an opium addict.

Poor Mr. Haddon went on living a day at a time doing his farm work, tending his garden and cutting wood. He stored some of his machinery under the overhanging rock on the road above his barn. He was a faithful attendant at the Presbyterian Church services and took up the Sunday offering.

The Haddons finally sold their property to Albert and Antoinette Ising from New York City, and they and their daughter Antoinette (Bubbins) lived there until they died. The Haddons went west to live with their son Charles, Jr. and family in the State of Washington. After living for a few years in Washington, Charlie and Orrie died and were buried there.

THE VILLAGE BELOW THE BRIDGE

For a few years, there was the Breakstone and Levine sub-station creamery on the left of the road just across the bridge. Here the farmers' milk was weighed, tested for butter fat and separated. The farmer brought his skimmed milk back home to give to his pigs and calves. The cream was taken to the large creamery in Windham to be churned into butter.

The creamery was a busy place mornings as many farmers were lined up with their horses and wagons and cans of milk to be processed. On their return home they usually would stop at the store for their mail, some groceries and to chat for a few minutes with anyone who wanted to talk. The creamery was a good place for us children on the way to school to stop in on cold winter mornings to get warm. The creamery closed probably about 1920; after that, farmers brought their milk to a platform by the garage and it was picked up by a big truck and taken to the Windham creamery.

Across the road from the creamery, Robert Peck built a new garage and installed gasoline pumps. Robert had married Gladys Davis, a school teacher from Hobart who had taught at East Jewett. They built a new house between the Vinings' and Grey's in the village.

Robert and Gladys had one daughter, Betty, who died while she was in high school. Robert was a skilled mechanic and soon established a prosperous business. For some years, he employed Edwin Garvey and Edwin Hitchcock as mechanics. After several years, Robert sold the garage to his employees and began working for the Greene County Highway Department. A few years later, while working, he suddenly died of a heart attack.

Edwin Garvey became sole owner of the garage and along with his son Ronny operated the business. Then, Ed died and Ronny continued with the garage for a number of years until he secured employment with the Greene County Highway Department as a mechanic and welder.

Below the garage was the Fred Rickard farm with a large house and a dairy barn, and below the creamery was the George Rickard home. The two brothers and their families lived across from one another for many years, with their brother Henry and wife Amy living up in the village.

THE VILLAGE SCHOOLHOUSE

The high steep bank behind the schoolhouse curved around to the road. In a pocket close to the bank and below the school was the home of Mrs. Sarah Johnson, a large widow, who lived there alone with no water source or toilet facilities. In the winter months, the snow would drift to a great depth between Mrs.

Johnson's little house and the foot of the steep hill. We boys would walk to the top of the hill behind the school and then along the ridge until we were behind Mrs. Johnson's house. At the high elevation above the house we would run, give a jump, fly through space and plunge down into the deep snow up to our hips and close to the house. Often it was difficult to work loose from the snow, but flying through the air was a thrilling, enjoyable experience.

For a long time, Mrs. Johnson, sitting in her front room by her little wood stove with her black smudged face and dirty apron, was unaware of the good times we were having at the rear of her home. When she discovered it, she notified the state police and our soaring abruptly ceased.

Those days in the little one-room rural school were wonderful days—carefree, innocent and happy, associating with boys and girls from neighboring homes. Mornings, children with their tin dinner pails could be seen walking from the farms and village homes to school.

There were a half dozen Hoyt children walking up the road from their home about a mile below the school; Charlie Williams with his watery eyes and thick glasses from the Round Hill road running to get to school before the bell rang; Gerald and Charlie Newcomb and their sisters Jessie and Norma coming down from their poor, old home way up on the Slater road. All came together in one simple, bare, wainscoted room to spend six hours learning to read, spell, write, do some simple arithmetic, and absorb a little history and geography at the feet of a great teacher—kind, firm and wise, who knew the meaning and importance of life. Playing during the day, eating lunch together under a tree or on a rock, learning to associate with others and to grow spiritually, mentally and physically made these children strong, capable men and women—contributing members of society. The teachers in the school for many years were Blanche Miller, Raymond Moseman and Abner Woodworth.

THE RICKARDS: HENRY, GEORGE AND FRED

The three Rickard brothers were home-loving men who kept to themselves and didn't participate in community life. They were fairly self-sufficient. Henry and Amy lived in the village below Gene Lewis' home. Henry had a slight speech defect. Amy was a faithful member of the Methodist Church. Henry did odd jobs and worked in the park summers. They had no children.

George and Julia's home was across the bridge below the village and close to the creek. George owned and operated a cider mill and each fall he was busy for several weeks making cider and vinegar for neighbors who brought him apples to be pressed into apple juice. Afternoons, on our way home from school, we children would stop at George's cider mill and he would give us sweet cider to drink in a dipper by the press. It was a great treat.

Summers, George had a productive and beautiful garden in the rich fertile soil east of their house and along the road. He grew quantities of vegetables and delicious, juicy strawberries and raspberries, all of which found a ready market. Julia had a bachelor brother, Levi Barnum, who was rather effeminate and had no home of his own. Levi could sew, cook, do housework and play the piano. He was pleasant, quite handsome and a good conversationalist.

Levi made his home for awhile with some of his many brothers and sisters, children of Bethuel. He worked in the house and did a little hard work on the farms. His favorite visiting places were with brother David and his family, brother Martin, brother George, sister Clara, but not often as long at her home as she was a diligent worker, spending as much time working in the barn as in the house.

It seemed that Levi's favorite home was with his sister Julia. Her home was quiet, orderly and pleasant. I recall stopping there one day after school, and Levi and Julia sat in the warm sunshine of their living room, rocking and conversing pleasantly. I don't recall ever seeing Levi working with George in his garden or cider mill. It was quite obvious that Levi preferred his sister's company to that of her husband.

George and Julia, who was a devoted Methodist, lived in their little home below the bridge until they both died. The third brother, Fred, was a cripple who had trouble walking in later years. Fred's wife Mae was a big, strong, healthy woman who had come from Ireland. She and Fred had five children—Alfred, Roger, Winfred, Clementina and Eunice. Eunice died when she was a little girl only seven or eight years old.

The Rickards lived on a nice little farm just below the store bridge and across the road from brother George. There was a large field between the farm and school where we played baseball and in winter coasted down the hill at the rear of the field. When the snow was crusted, we could go way across the field to the road next to the creek. The farm was large enough to support a team of horses and several cows. With milk and butter from the dairy and an abundance of vegetables from the garden, the family lived well and the children were healthy and strong.

The family's income was earned by Fred's drawing stove wood for local farmers to private homes in Windham and Hensonville. Mae, who was ambitious and husky, had plenty of work helping housewives with their cleaning and regular household work at a dollar a day. As the children grew older, they, too, earned money picking berries, doing odd jobs and running errands.

Alfred worked for local farmers and then, while in his early 20's, left to go West. He never returned home and never wrote, just disappeared.

Clementina, like her mother, worked in many homes and finally went into the restaurant business for herself. For several years before her death, she and her husband Hugh Salisbury owned and operated Salsibury Inn, the former Roswell Vining home, a popular eating place between Maplecrest and Hensonville, now known as the Harp and Eagle Restaurant.

Roger, while in grade school, demonstrated business acumen. His first ventures were buying calves from the farmers and selling them again. Soon, he had a small truck and was in the business speculating in cattle. He prospered and expanded his business.

His brother Winfred, also ambitious and a worker, was soon working with Roger. They enlarged the home barn, acquired a dairy herd, began sending milk to the creamery. They purchased farm equipment, including tractors, hay bailers, plows and wagons. Soon, the brothers were renting other farms and then buying them. Hay was cut and drawn to feed the many cattle from as far away as Windham. The Van Loan farm on Round Hill was bought and the big DeLong farm of several hundred acres in East Jewett was also purchased. The stables on these farms were filled with cattle being bought and sold from as far away as Delaware County.

Roger did much of the cattle business and Winfred, who was skilled in farm work and operating farm machinery, managed the farms. Winfred, in addition to plowing and harrowing the fields, mowing and bailing hay, also drove the big trucks loaded with cattle being bought and sold. Roger married and had two sons, but in middle age became ill and died. His wife, Dora, sold the home farm and the equipment was sold at a sale.

George and Julia had passed away and Winfred and his wife Irene purchased his Uncle George's place across the road from the childhood farm where Fred and his family had lived. Winfred and Irene are the only remaining Rickards living in Maplecrest.

THE BIG HOLLOW MEN'S CLUB

In the early days of the present century in small rural settlements, there were few newspapers and magazines and, of course, no radios or televisions. School attendance was not required. Very few children obtained more than a fourth- or fifth-grade education. Children learned to read, write, spell and do simple arithmetic, which completed their formal education. Securing the basic necessities of life with no labor-saving devices required hard work by all members of a family—husbands, wives and children. It was work from sun-up to sun-down with practically no social life.

Gus Moseman was an intelligent, versatile man—a good businessman, a promoter and public-spirited individual. Gus got the idea of easily providing some recreation and social life for the men on the farms and in the village of Big Hollow by organizing a men's club. He imagined that such a group might meet one evening a week, possibly on Saturday, with individuals bringing some refreshments from home, such as sandwiches, cake, cookies or a pie. Coffee could be made at the meeting place. Games such as dominoes, checkers and cards could be played. The young men might even wish to wrestle or box. And, of course, there would be opportunity for just sitting around, reading and chatting with one's neighbors about people, work and the activities in the Valley.

Gus' idea appealed to the men. The Club was organized with Gus as the leader. On the road just above the store and across from the John Irish house was a building lot. It was decided to construct a club house on this location.

The men went to work with enthusiasm and diligence building a rectangular club house around 24 feet by 36 feet in size.

Among the twenty or more men interested in the club were Raymond Moseman, a school teacher; Henry Distin, a farmer and Sunday school teacher; Romaine Law and William Henry Moseman, the local postmaster and merchant; Charlie Phelps, a lumberman; Roswell Vining, Dwight and Will Hitchcock and Jake Planck, farmers; Will Vining and Walter Bray, businessmen; Merritt and Vernon DeLong and George Winchell, laboring men; Harold Hitchcock, a high school student; and several others. The Club immediately proved to be very popular. The men looked forward to a pleasant, relaxing evening with friends and neighbors. In all likelihood, many wives and children enjoyed an evening at home by themselves. The Club was good for the community as it brought the men together and they became better acquainted with one another and therefore more understanding and compassionate neighbors. The moral and spiritual life of the homes and community grew better because of the Club. The group also organized a men's Bible class and met on Sundays in the Methodist Church. Interest grew and attendance was excellent.

Unfortunately, there were members in the club as are often found in families and groups of any kind—those who were envious and jealous of the leadership and the person in charge. No matter how meek and unassuming a leader may be and how much he tries to remain in the background, the very success and growth of the group attests to the leader's ability and character. So it was with Gus and the Big Hollow Men's Club. A few in the group became envious of Gus' leadership and the Club's popularity. A new leader was elected who did not possess leadership qualities. Interest and attendance began to dwindle and the Club soon died. Later, the building served as the house where Frank and Minnie Palmer lived for several years. The old building still stands but is now unoccupied. It is a reminder of the jealous nature of man.

THE BIG HOLLOW STORE AND POST OFFICE

The location of the store and post office, which were in the same large building, was strategic. It was at the western end of the Hollow and Village street. On the right was county route 40 going up the mountain to East Jewett and Tannersville. On its left was the bridge and route 40 leading to Hensonville, State Route 23 and the outside world.

Since the first settler arrived in Big Hollow in 1795, there probably was some kind of a trading post or crude cabin-like store at the site of the present store and post office as early as 1820. The first Big Hollow postmaster, Friend Holcomb, was appointed on January 31, 1829. So it seems reasonable to believe that the first store and post office were in the same building at this important intersection of the three roads as early as 1830.

According to the autobiography of Sherwood A. Moseman, Mr. Moseman's father Robert and Uncle William Henry Moseman rebuilt the store around 1850 with capital of only one hundred dollars. Their first stock was a sugar barrel full of groceries. The front of the store commanded a full view of everyone entering the valley from either the west or the south and anyone leaving the valley passed by. Also, the full length of the village street was clearly visible from the store.

William Henry Moseman and Sherwood (Gus) Moseman owned and operated the store for nearly 75 years. Romaine Law owned it later for a few years. Then, from 1925 until 1965, Valentine W. Morrow owned and operated the store and served as postmaster during those years.

Val and Irene, his wife, improved the store in many ways. A very nice apartment was built upstairs. The post office was enlarged and improved. These were good years for Val and Irene and for the community at large. A spirit of friendship, neighborliness, good will and cooperation prevailed throughout the entire valley.

In order to meet many of the needs of its customers, a wide variety of goods were carried in the store. There were nails, hammers and axes; boots, shoes, clothing, cloth, needles and thread; patent medicines, laxatives, iodine, headache tablets, cough syrups, and, of course, a full line of basic groceries, such as flour, sugar, molasses, and kerosene; a candy case with a wide assortment of penny candy; also smoking and chewing tobacco and a few cigars.

Some customers traded eggs and butter or even stove wood for merchandise. Liberal credit was available to those who needed it. Occasionally cash was paid. If not, many bills were paid at the end of the month or when the customers could scrape together enough money to settle their accounts. Then, there were a few bills that were never paid, or a neighbor settled them.

The strategic location of the store and post office with everyone entering and leaving the valley passing by it, and with the store and post office together in the same building, made the place an important and busy community center. Children on their way to and from school would stop at the store for a pencil or a penny candy. And we boys enjoyed crawling up through the underground tunnel created by a brook that flowed underneath the store. The women in the street, up the hill and below the bridge would walk to the store for a cake of borax soap, a spool of thread or some other commodity, pick up the mail and pass the time of day with the neighbors.

During the long winter evenings, some of the men in the village and farmers Ros Vining and Will Hitchcock would meet in the store around the big pot-bellied stove to play a game of dominoes known as ''42.'' The game is much like pinochle. Four men would hold a Nabisco metal sign as a table on their knees and play the game. Sometimes two games would be played at the same time. Often, retired men in the village would meet in the store in the afternoon and again after supper to play. It is an exciting, enjoyable game which one never tires of playing. After playing for 70 years, I still look forward to an occasion when our daughter Linda and granddaughter Kathy come to play with us as many as six games in one evening.

The men playing 42 in the store tended to make the atmosphere pleasant and restful. In summer, the soda fountain attracted many people. Ice cream and soft drinks such as birch beer, ginger ale and sarsaparilla were sold. Ice cream sold for a nickel a cone and soft drinks for a nickel a bottle.

The store was not only an important economic center but an important social center as well. It was a strong bond holding the inhabitants and community together in a friendly, brotherly group.